100 WAYS YOUR TWO-YEAR-OLD CAN HURT YOU

COMICS TO EASE THE STRESS OF PARENTING

CHEN WENG

Andrews McMeel
PUBLISHING®

Andrews McMeel Publishing
a division of Andrews McMeel Universal
1130 Walnut Street, Kansas City, Missouri 64106
www.andrewsmcmeel.com

20 21 22 23 24 TEN 10 9 8 7 6 5 4 3 2 1

ISBN: 978-1-5248-5563-5

Library of Congress Control Number: 2019956543

Editor: Lucas Wetzel
Art Director: Sierra Stanton
Production Editor: Amy Strassner
Production Manager: Tamara Haus

ATTENTION: SCHOOLS AND BUSINESSES

Andrews McMeel books are available at quantity discounts with bulk purchase for educational, business, or sales promotional use. For information, please e-mail the Andrews McMeel Publishing Special Sales Department: specialsales@amuniversal.com.

To my family.
Thanks for letting me make fun of you,
and for the inspiration.

Contents

AS A CHILD

AS A TEENAGER

AS A YOUNG ADULT

AFTER HAVING KIDS

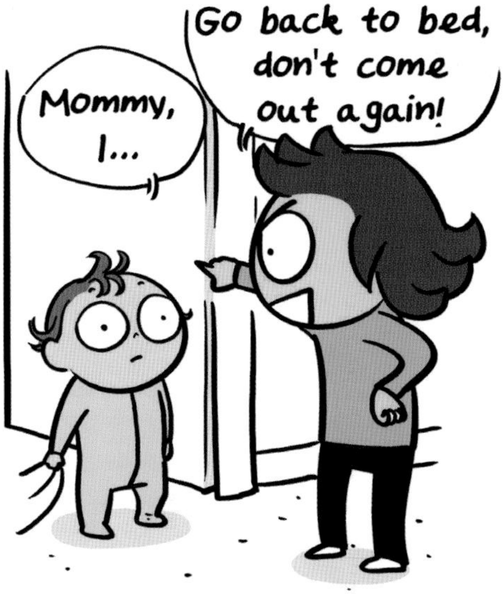
Mommy, I...
Go back to bed, don't come out again!

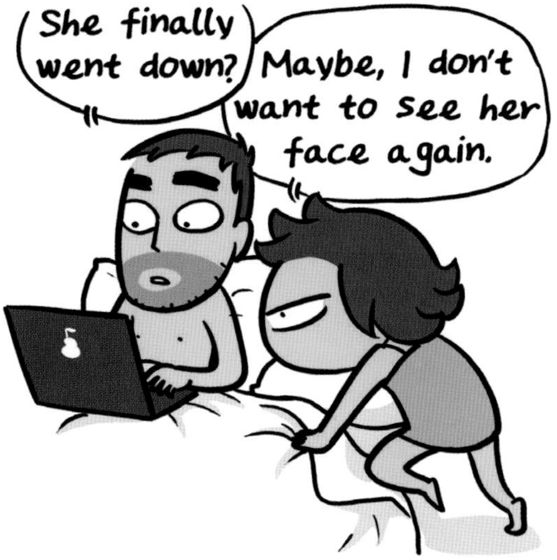
She finally went down?
Maybe, I don't want to see her face again.

FIVE MINUTES LATER

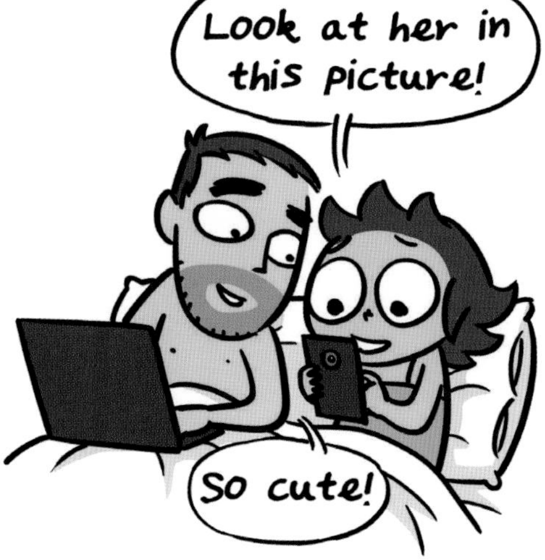
Look at her in this picture!
So cute!

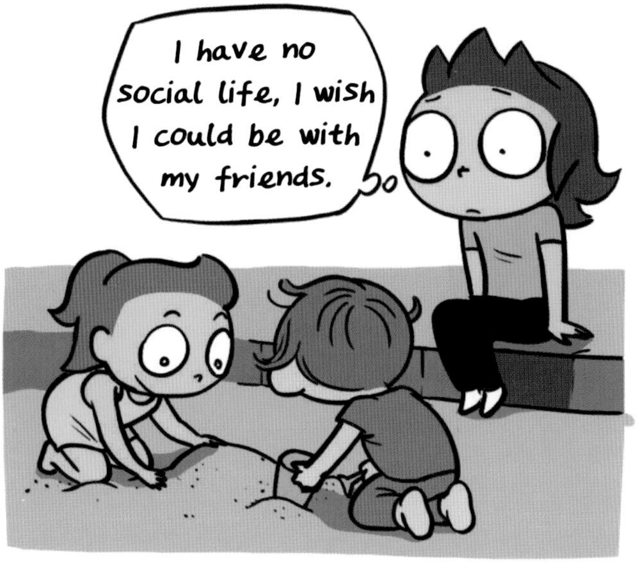
I have no social life, I wish I could be with my friends.

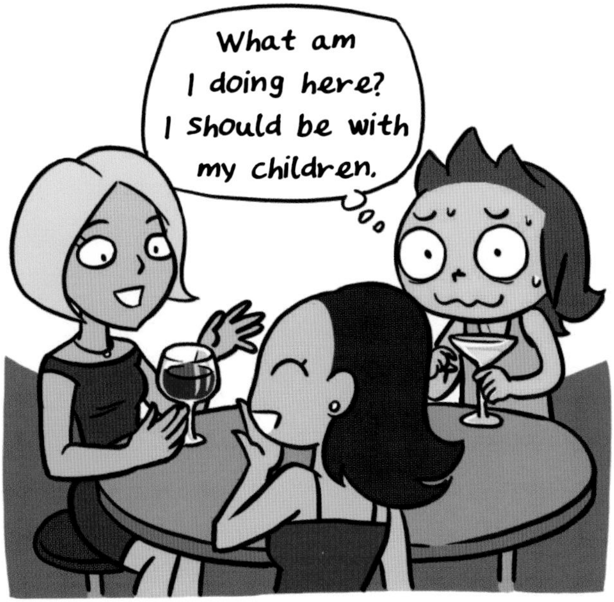
What am I doing here? I should be with my children.

OTHER PEOPLE

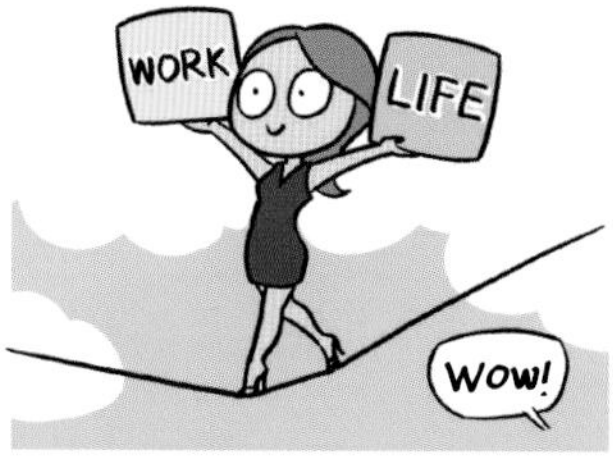
WORK
LIFE
Wow!

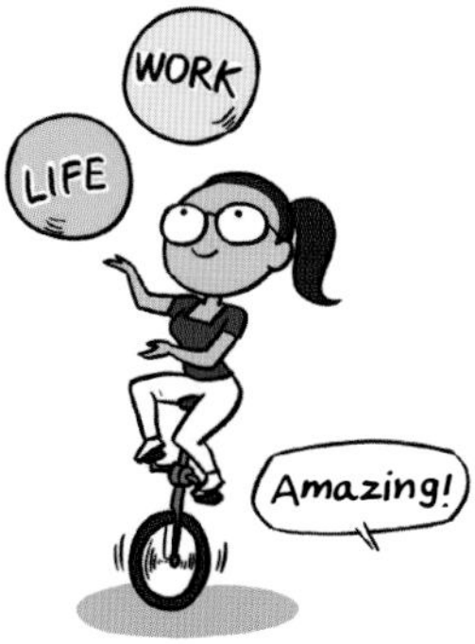
WORK
LIFE
Amazing!

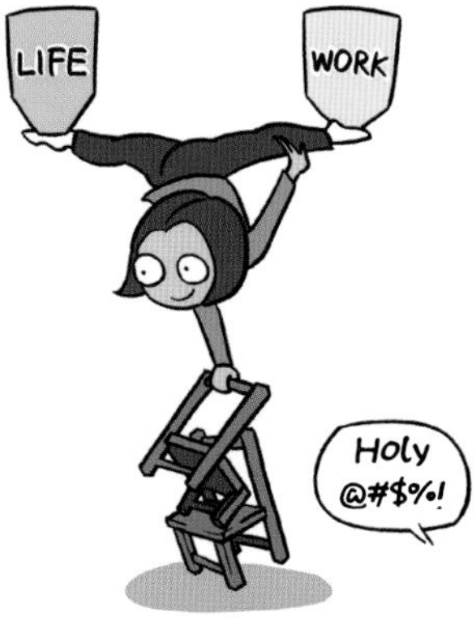
LIFE
WORK
Holy @#$%!

ME

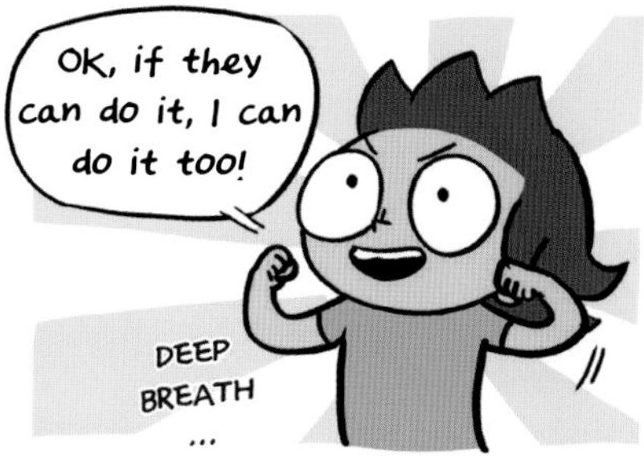
Ok, if they can do it, I can do it too!
DEEP BREATH ...

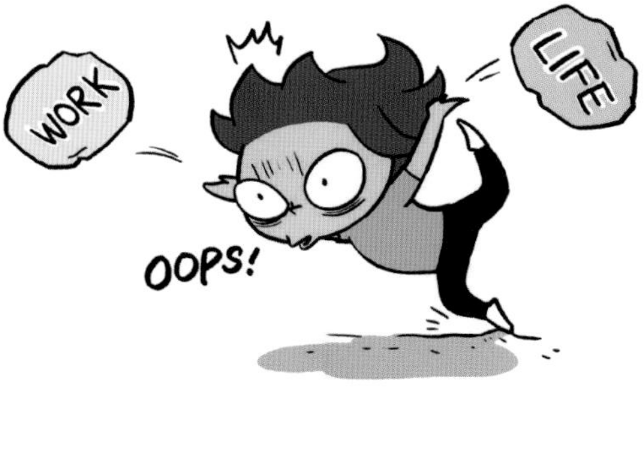
WORK
LIFE
OOPS!

BEFORE KIDS

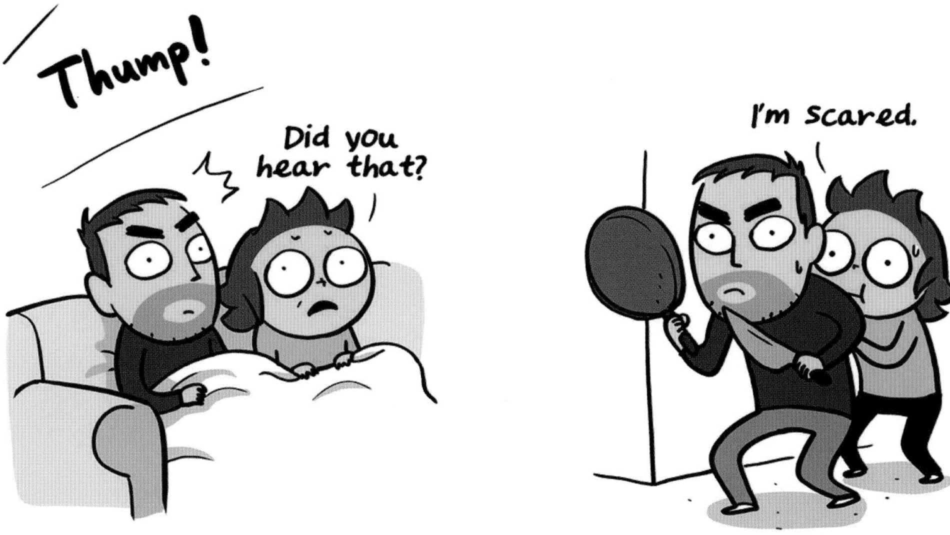
Thump!
Did you hear that?
I'm scared.

AFTER KIDS

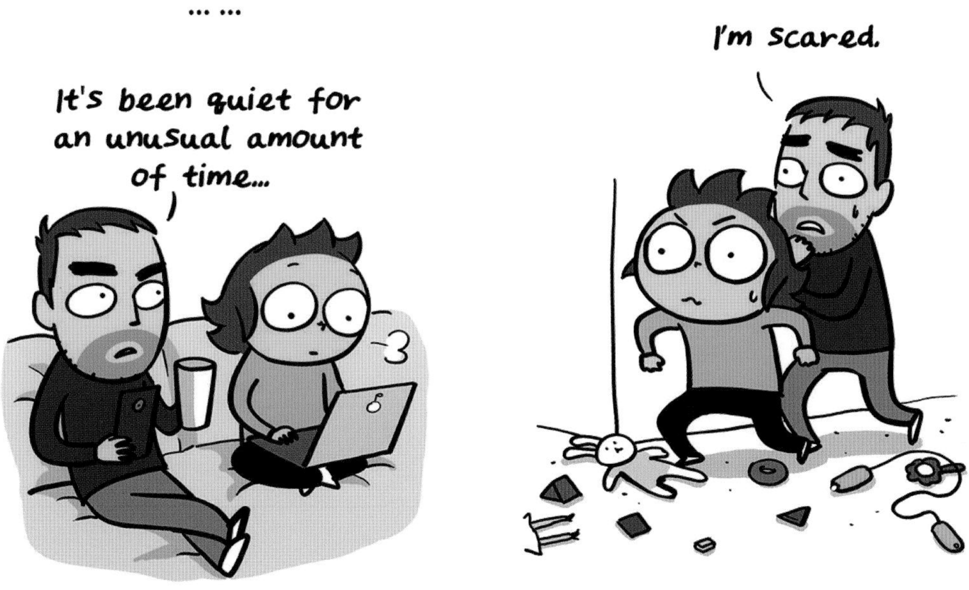
... ...
It's been quiet for an unusual amount of time...
I'm scared.

FIVE YEARS OLD

FIFTEEN YEARS OLD

TWENTY YEARS OLD

EARLY THIRTIES

LATE THIRTIES

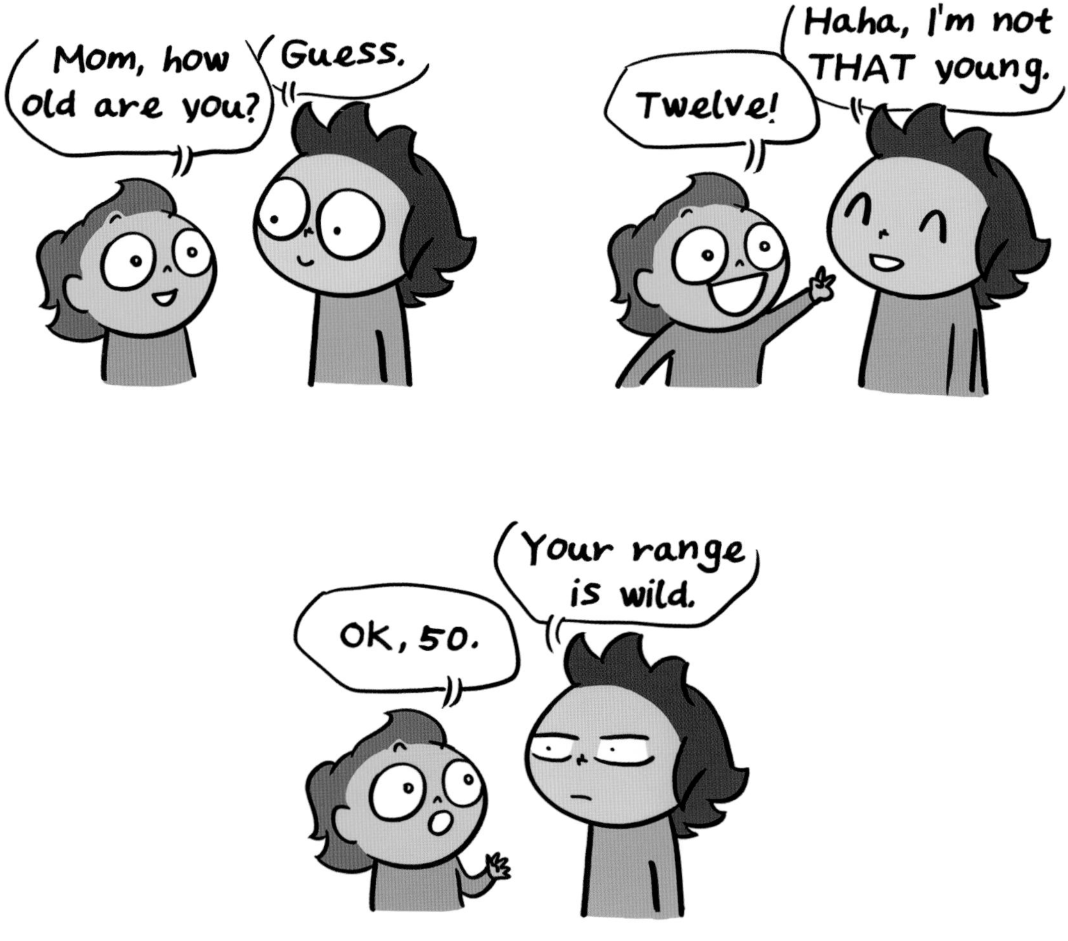
Mom, how old are you?
Guess.
Twelve!
Haha, I'm not THAT young.
OK, 50.
Your range is wild.

GOING TO A RESTAURANT BEFORE MY KIDS' NAPS

A DISASTER

GOING TO A RESTAURANT AFTER MY KIDS' NAPS

A GOOD TIME

WHEN I PUT MY CHILD
TO SLEEP

WHEN I ACTUALLY
GO TO SLEEP

I need to find a goal
for myself. Guess I
should have kids...

TWO KIDS LATER

Now I need to find
goals for all of us.

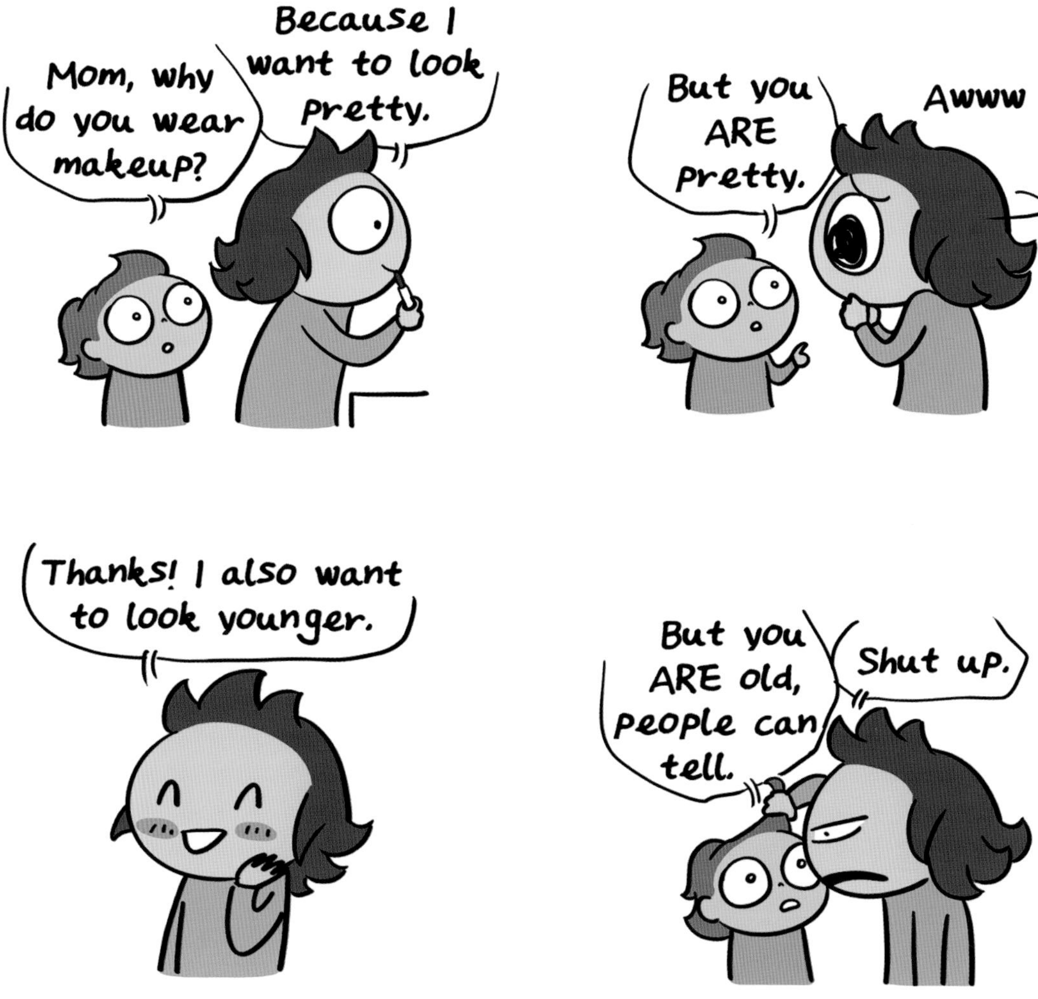
Mom, why do you wear makeup?
Because I want to look pretty.
But you ARE pretty.
Awww
Thanks! I also want to look younger.
But you ARE old, people can tell.
Shut up.

Aww, she is so cute.

Kiss

Sniff
Sniff

Mommy?

Huh?

Stop!

WHEN I'M COOKING

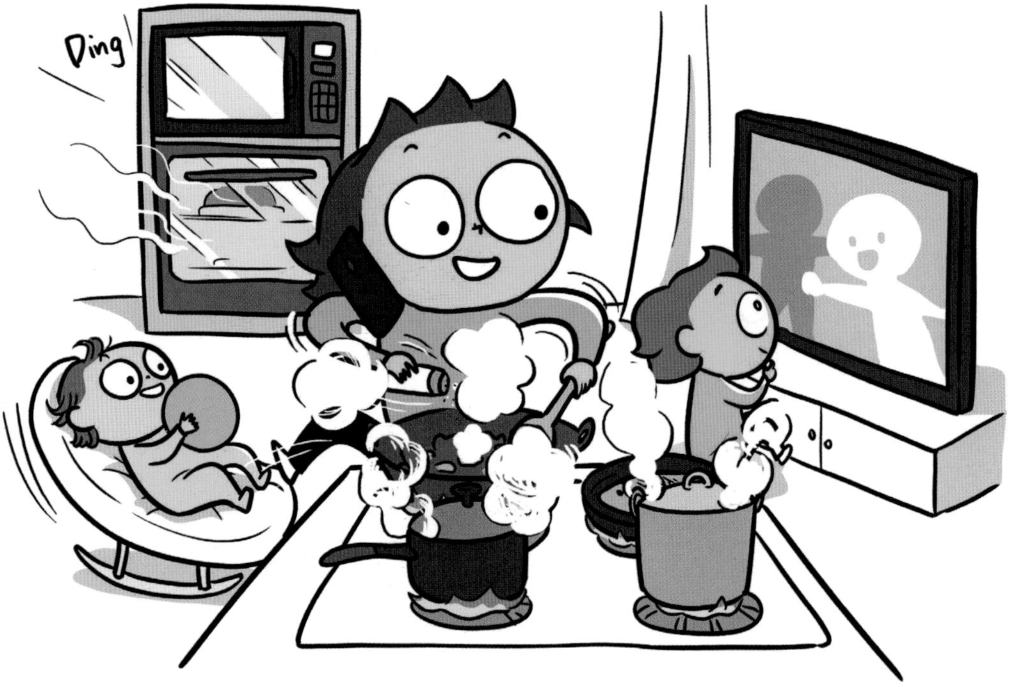
Ding

WHEN MY HUSBAND IS COOKING

WHEN MOM DRESSES THE KIDS

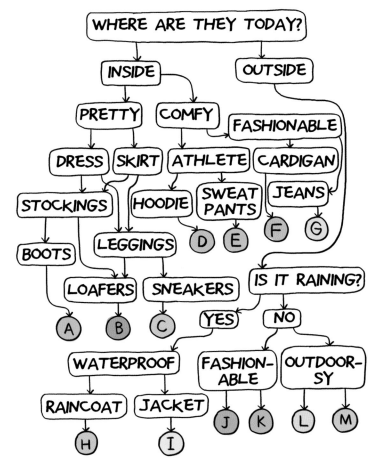

LETTERS MEAN DIFFERENT COMBINATIONS.

WHEN DAD DRESSES THE KIDS

ARE THEY COVERED BY CLOTHING?

YES

NO

COVER THEM WITH CLOTHING

DONE!

WHEN GRANDMA DRESSES THE KIDS

IS IT COLD?

YES

NO

BUT I FEEL COLD

WEAR MORE

WHEN MY HUSBAND IS DRIVING

WHEN I'M DRIVING

MY HUSBAND'S OFFICE

MY OFFICE

MY HUSBAND'S CAR

MY CAR

THE POWER OF LOVE

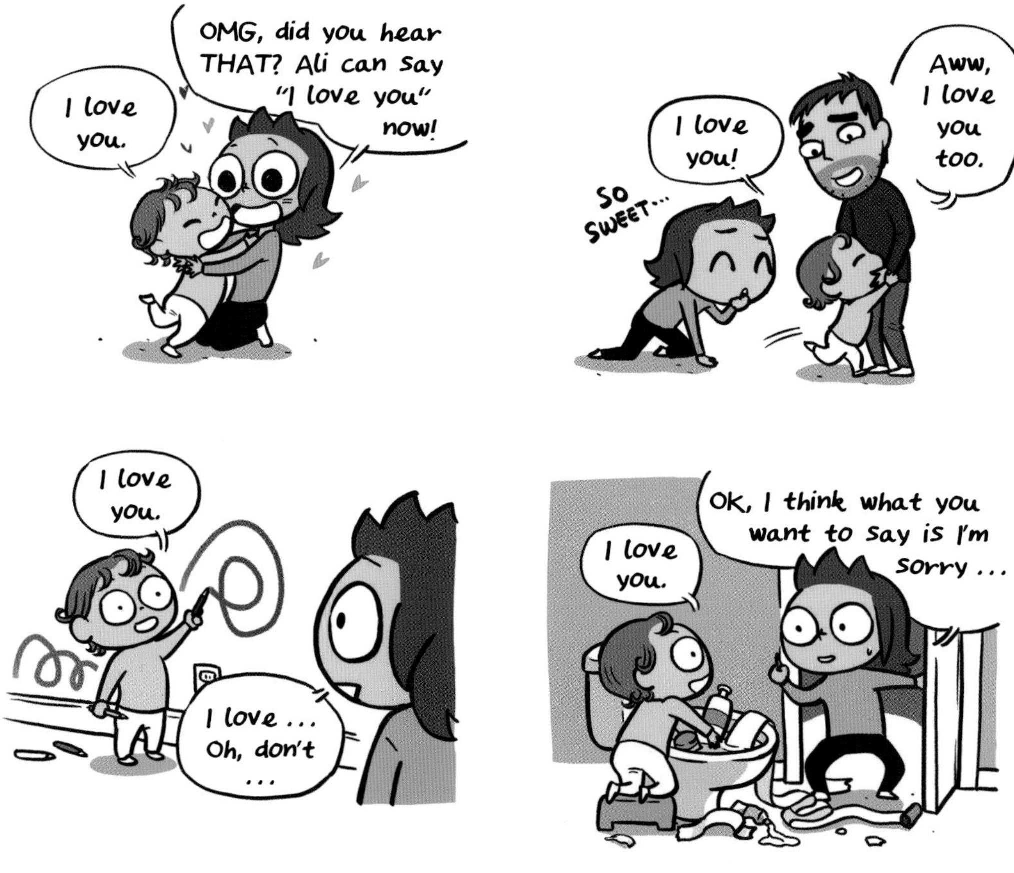
I love you.
OMG, did you hear THAT? Ali can say "I love you" now!
SO SWEET...
I love you!
Aww, I love you too.
I love you.
I love ... Oh, don't ...
I love you.
OK, I think what you want to say is I'm sorry ...

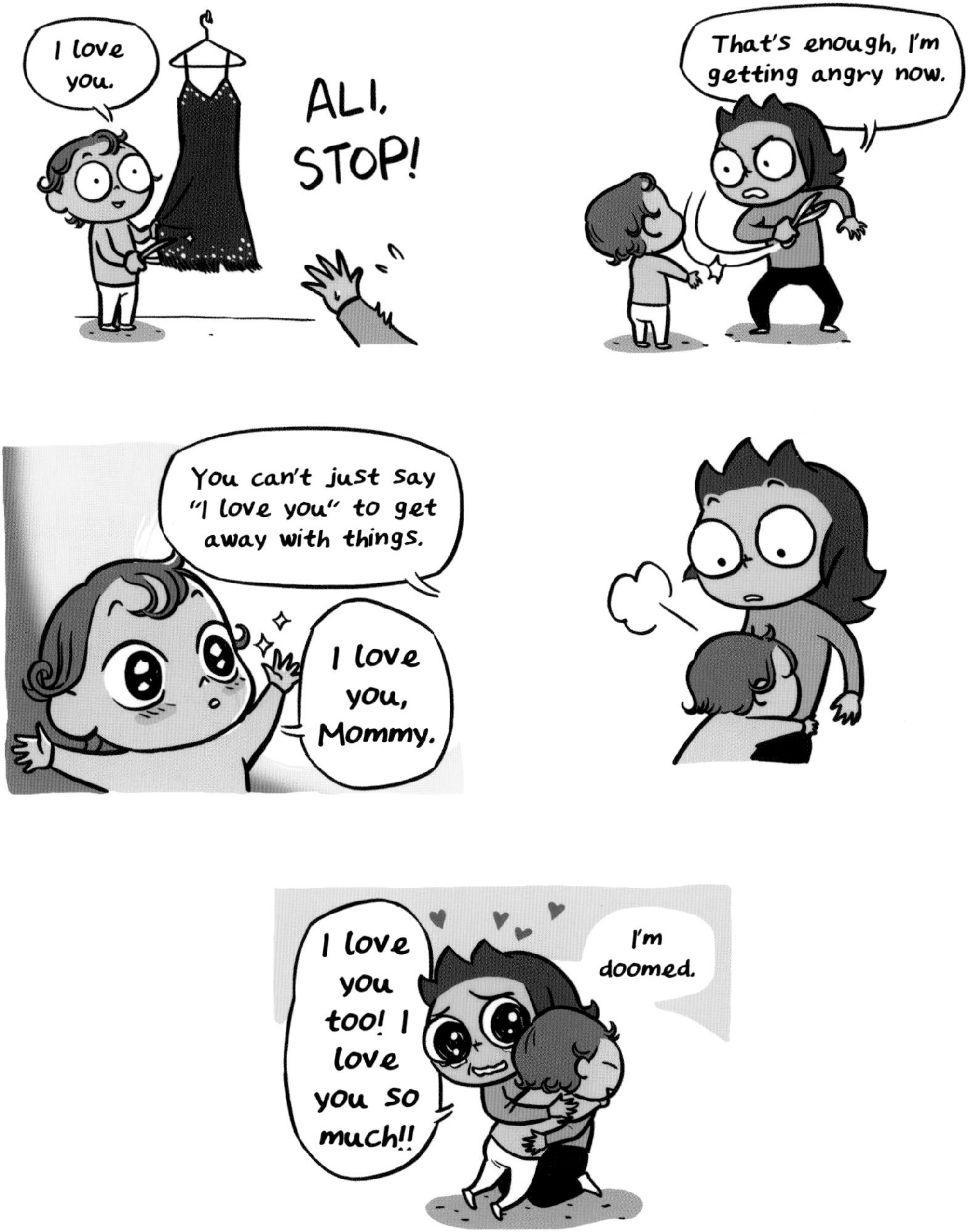
I love you.
ALI, STOP!
That's enough, I'm getting angry now.
You can't just say "I love you" to get away with things.
I love you, Mommy.
I love you too! I love you so much!!
I'm doomed.

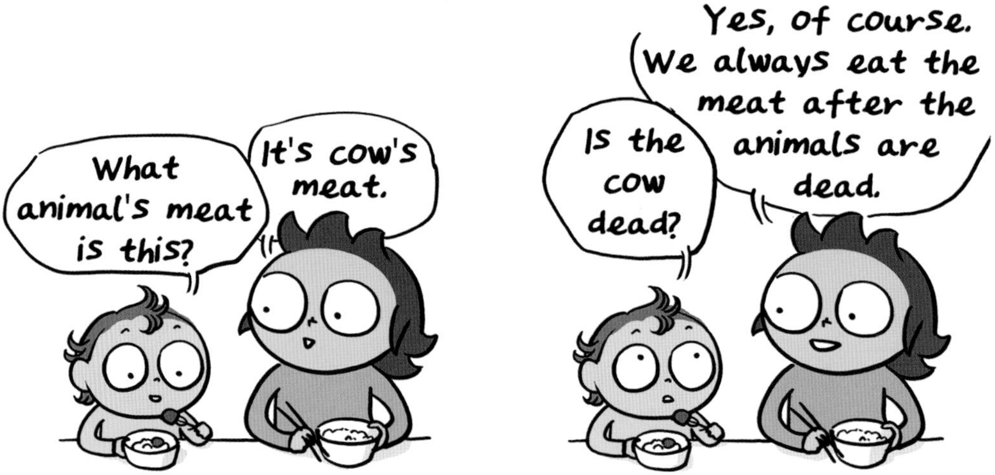
What animal's meat is this?
It's cow's meat.
Is the cow dead?
Yes, of course. We always eat the meat after the animals are dead.

LATER

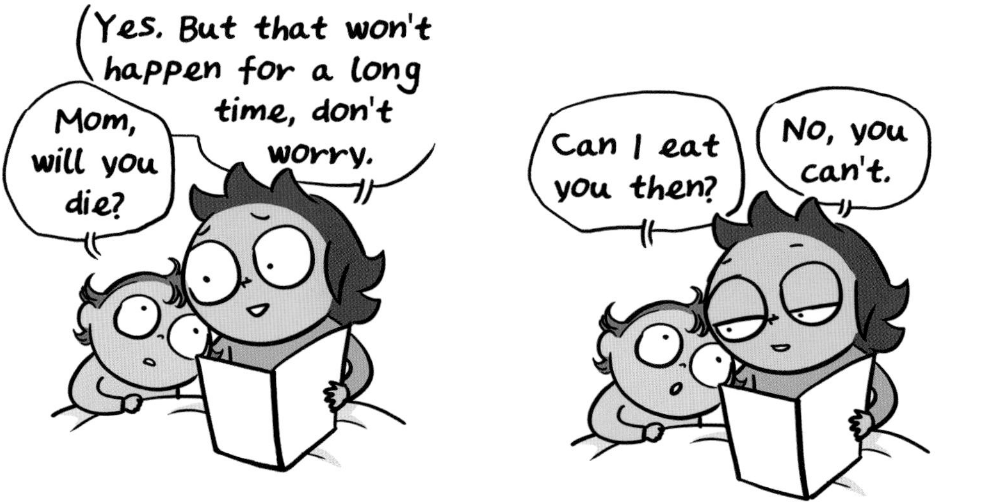
Mom, will you die?
Yes. But that won't happen for a long time, don't worry.
Can I eat you then?
No, you can't.

MY KIDS' NATURAL EXPRESSIONS

MY KIDS' EXPRESSIONS WHEN I'M TAKING PICTURES

PREGNANCY

FIRSTBORN

I only eat food with high protein and low carbs. Going to have a healthy baby!

SECOND-BORN

I'M EATING WHATEVER THE HECK I WANT.

FEEDING

FIRSTBORN

MAKE FRESH FOOD DAILY, ALL ORGANIC.

Everything that goes into my baby has to be the best!

SECOND-BORN

I found this in the fridge and warmed it up for you. Just cry if it's bad.

FEVER

FIRSTBORN

HURRY! CALL THE DOCTOR! CALL 911!

Calm down.

SECOND-BORN

Need to call the doctor when it's 103°F. Now it's just 102°F. I will wait and see.

CHILD'S PROGRESS

FIRSTBORN

Wow, come look at this! Our baby might be gifted!

Rocket.

AMAZING!

SECOND-BORN

Look, Mom!

That's nice. Now come have dinner.

NURSING

FIRSTBORN

Why don't I have enough milk, why doesn't she latch, why does it hurt so much ... I need to hang in there!

SECOND-BORN

I don't produce enough milk, sorry! Here is your bottle.

CLOTHES

FIRSTBORN

You sure we need so many?

Yes! I'm dressing her up every day!

← Hasn't been born yet

SECOND-BORN

Honey, I think she needs new clothes.

Nah, she can wear her sister's soon.

PARENTING

FIRSTBORN

SECOND-BORN

THE FIRST DAY OF SCHOOL

FIRSTBORN

SECOND-BORN

Birthdays are the best thing EVER!

Do you know Mommy's birthday is coming after yours?

OH!!

Happy birthday, Mommy!!

It's not for four months.

Happy birthday!!

It's not today ...

Happy birthday!!
No!!
You know, I'm just not excited about my birthday like you.
Why?
Because I'm getting old.
But will you still be my mommy?
Yes, I'll always be your mommy, even when I'm very very old.
Yay! I want a strawberry cake!

STEP 1:
TELL THEM IT'S TIME TO LEAVE

STEP 2:
TELL THEM AGAIN

STEP 3:
PUT ON THEIR CLOTHES

STEP 4:
LOOK FOR THE WATER BOTTLE

STEP 5:
CHANGE THEIR CLOTHES

STEP 6:
PUT ON THEIR SHOES

STEP 7:
LIE DOWN

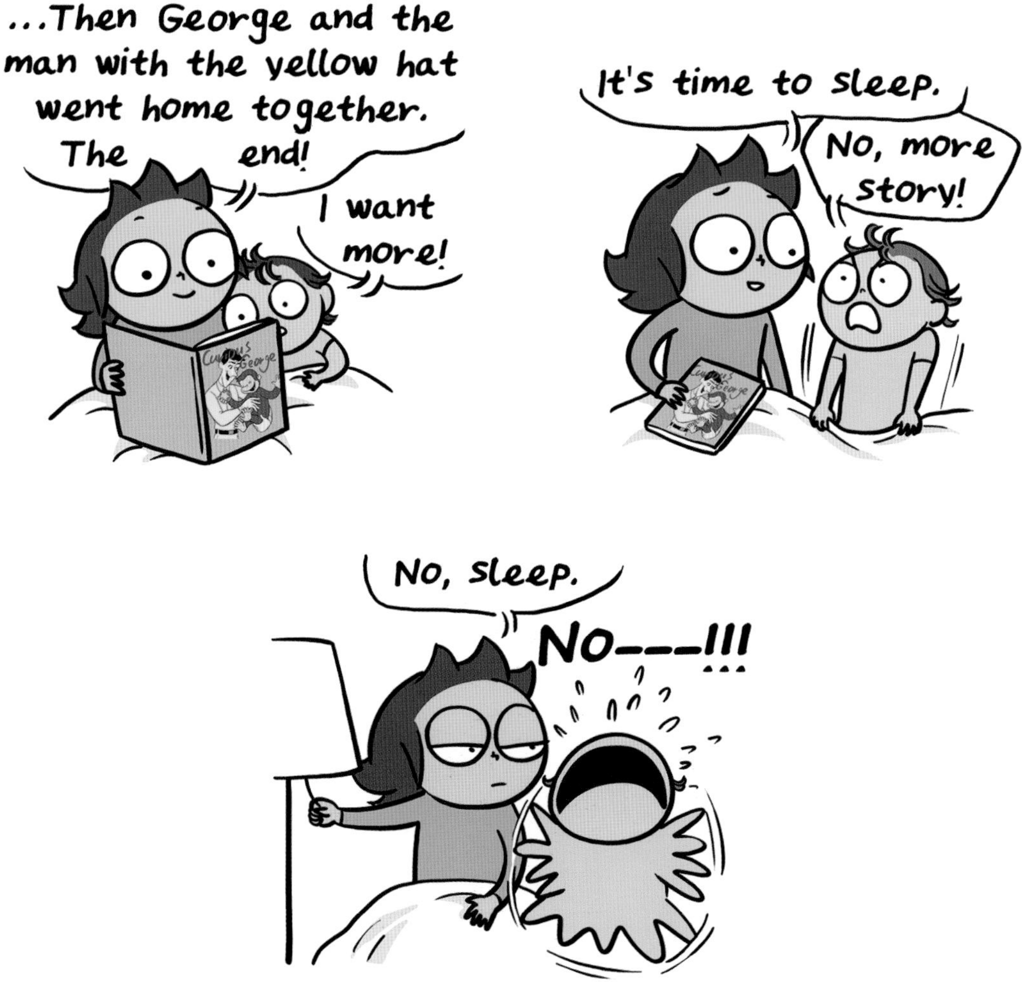
...Then George and the man with the yellow hat went home together. The end!
I want more!
It's time to sleep.
No, more story!
No, sleep.
NO---!!!

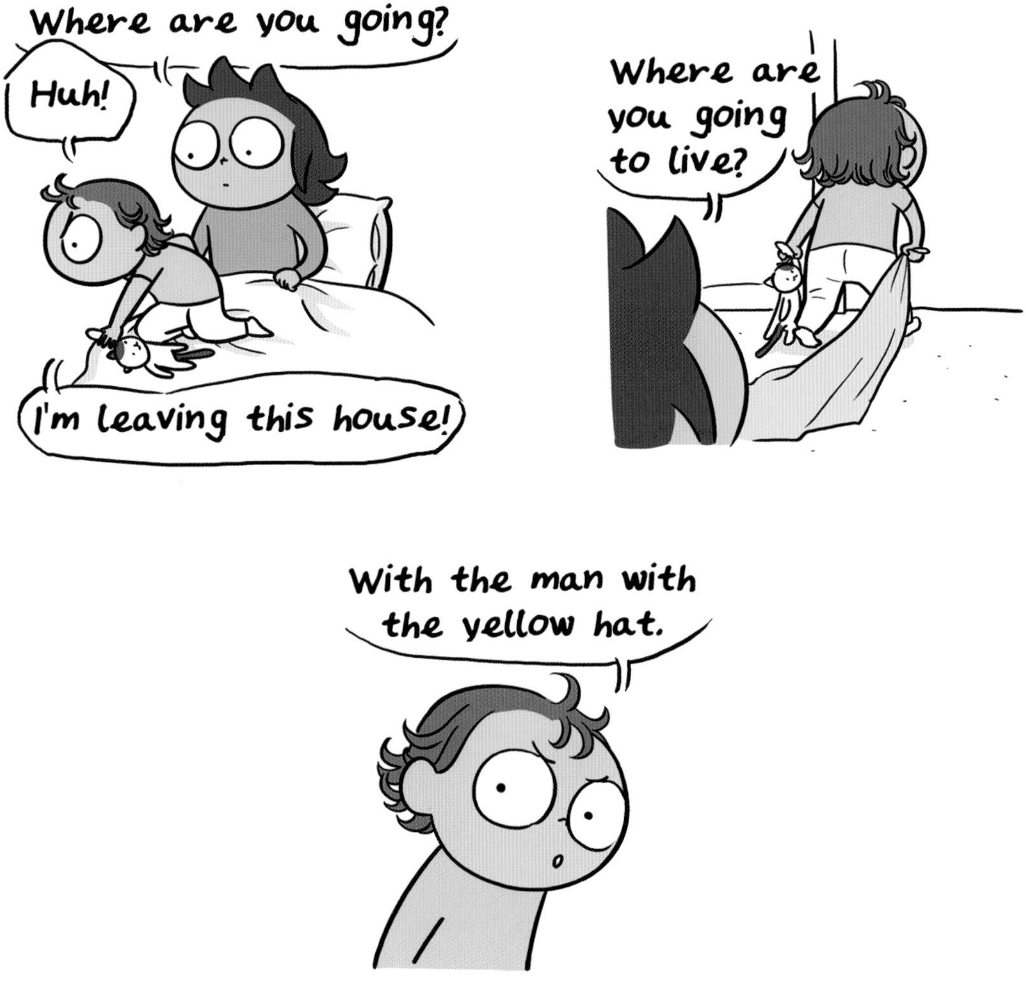
Where are you going?
Huh!
I'm leaving this house!
Where are you going to live?
With the man with the yellow hat.

PLACES WHERE ALI LIKES TO PUT HER HANDS

DOORJAMBS

IN ELECTRICAL
SOCKETS

WINDOW GAPS

THE BACK LEG
OF A CAT

UNDER THE
TIPPING CHAIR

INSIDE OF A
PUBLIC TOILET
BOWL

BEHIND THE
BICYCLE WHEEL

AN OPENED
MOUTH

IS THE MAN WHO I GAVE A NOTE
TO FOR THE THREE THINGS TO
BUY FROM THE STORE

WHO CALLED ME WHILE
AT THE STORE

THEN BROUGHT BACK A
LOT OF EXTRA STUFF

BUT NOT THE THING I WANTED

Click!

Sigh

What's wrong?

I look old and ugly.

Mom, even if you are old and ugly, I still love you.

ME WHEN I WAS YOUNG

What's your drive for working hard?

To live the ideal life! To have a house, a car, and the love of my life. Achieving my dreams, and devoting myself to the betterment of the human race!

ME NOW

What's your drive for working hard?

Anxiety. Total anxiety.

Put the cover on, it's cold.

No, I'm not cold!

How come?

Really! Mom, look at this!

See? I have hair.

Finish your food.

No, I'm full!

FIVE MINUTES LATER

Have some ice cream!

You said you were full. How can you have room for ice cream?

The stomach for dinner is full, but the stomach for ice cream is empty.

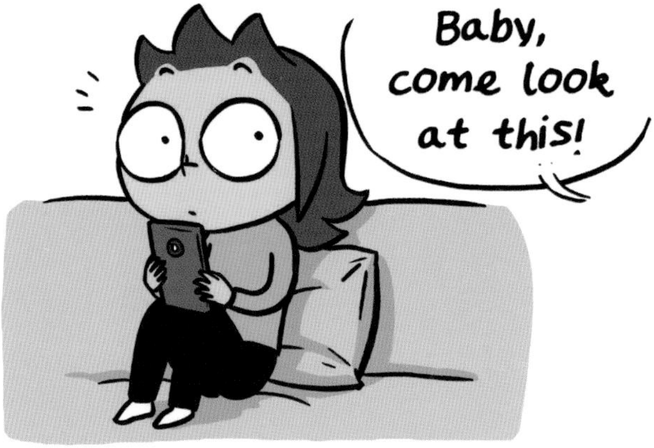
Baby, come look at this!

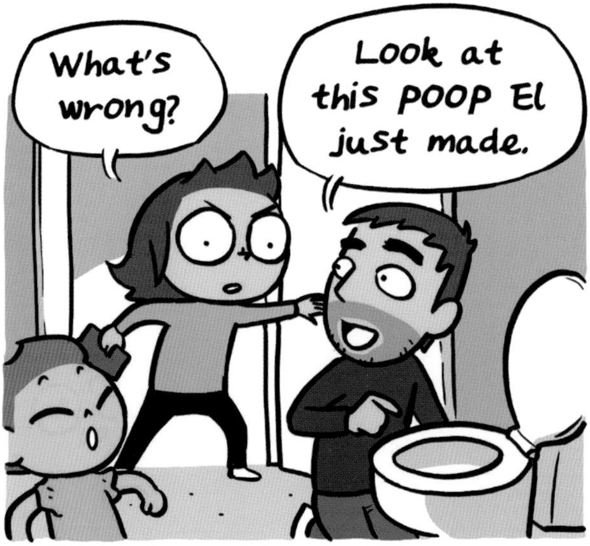
What's wrong?
Look at this POOP El just made.

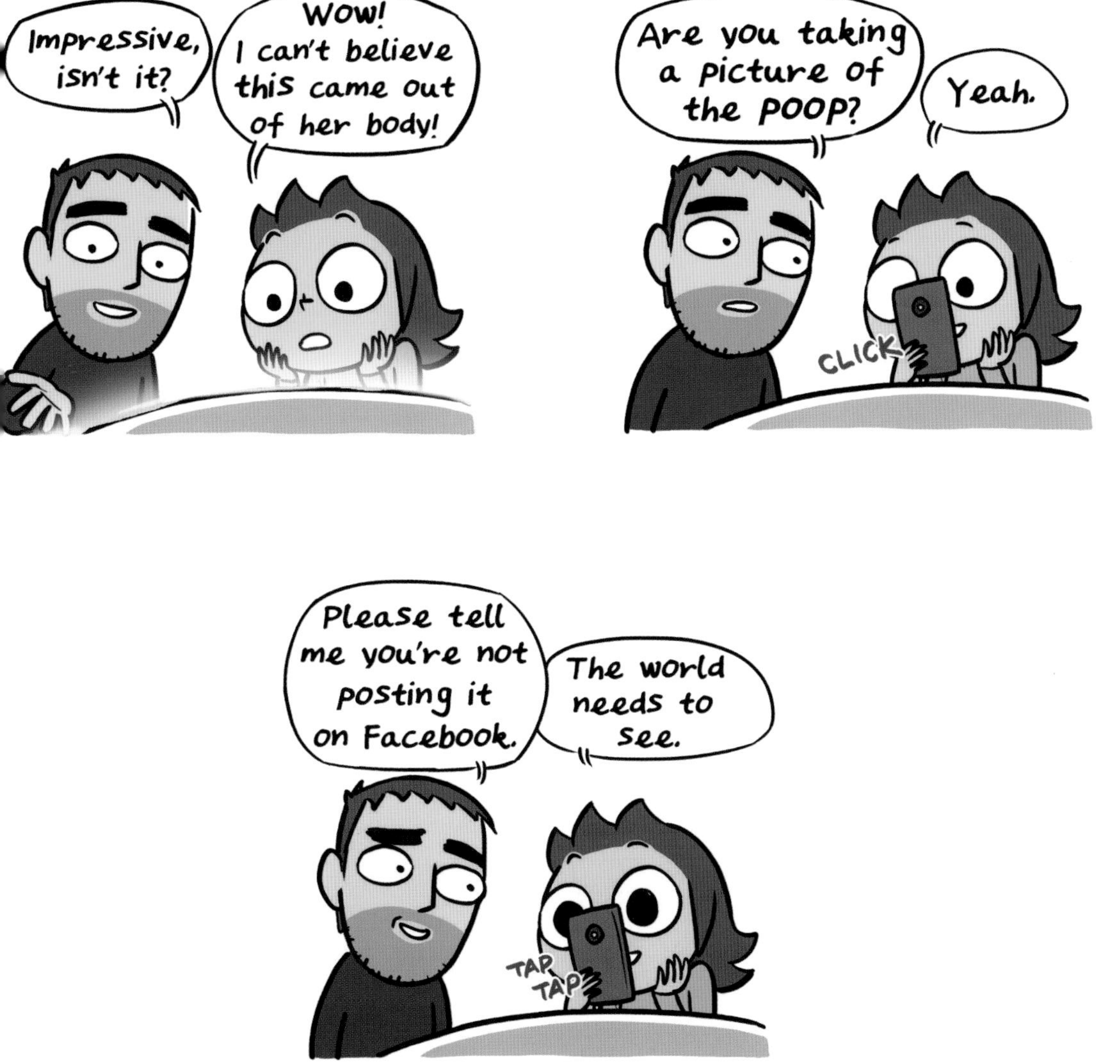
Impressive, isn't it?
WOW! I can't believe this came out of her body!
Are you taking a picture of the POOP?
Yeah.
CLICK
Please tell me you're not posting it on Facebook.
The world needs to see.
TAP TAP

My son can do
a backflip.

My daughter can
speak three languages.

My son can play
Mozart.

My daughter goes
to sleep on her own.

How do you
do that?
TEACH US!

42

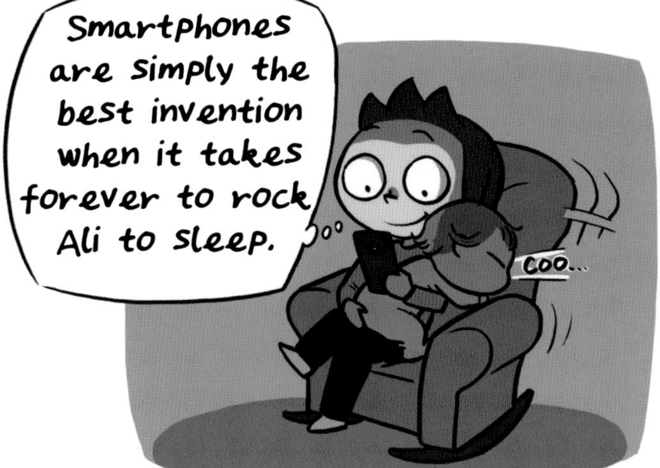
Smartphones are simply the best invention when it takes forever to rock Ali to sleep.
COO...

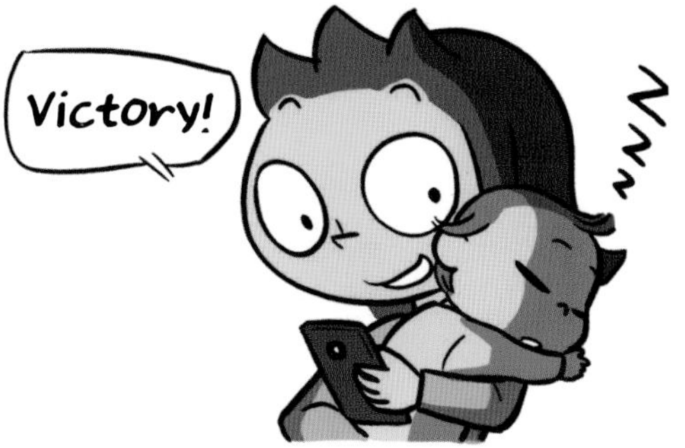
Victory!
ZZZ

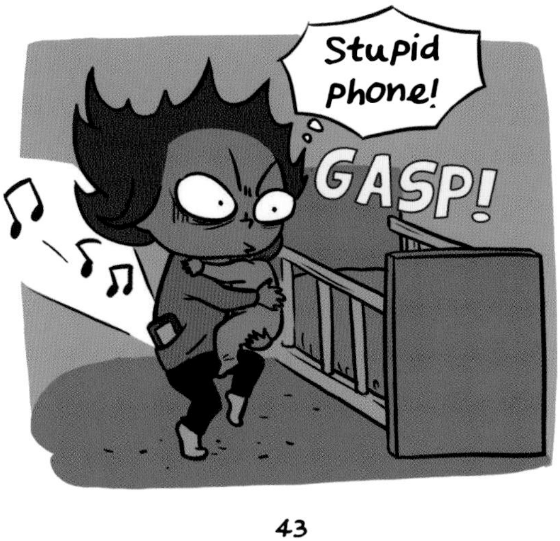
Stupid phone!
GASP!

MY FRIENDS

FIRSTBORN

SECOND-BORN

BABY PICTURES

FIRSTBORN

SECOND-BORN

IN THE PHONE

IN THE CLOUD

TOYS

FIRSTBORN

SECOND-BORN

EARLY LEARNING ACTIVITIES

FIRSTBORN

SECOND-BORN

HYGIENE

FIRSTBORN

Everything that touches the baby needs to be washed, sterilized, and air-dried.

SECOND-BORN

Look, she's licking the floor.

Haha, funny.

INSPIRATION

FIRSTBORN

Hmm, interesting.

SECOND-BORN

Hmm, interesting.

MY STATUS

FIRSTBORN

SECOND-BORN

MY WALLET

FIRSTBORN

SECOND-BORN

ONE YEAR OLD

THREE YEARS OLD

WHEN I SLEEP FOR
SIX HOURS

WHEN I SLEEP FOR
EIGHT HOURS

WHEN I SLEEP FOR
TEN HOURS

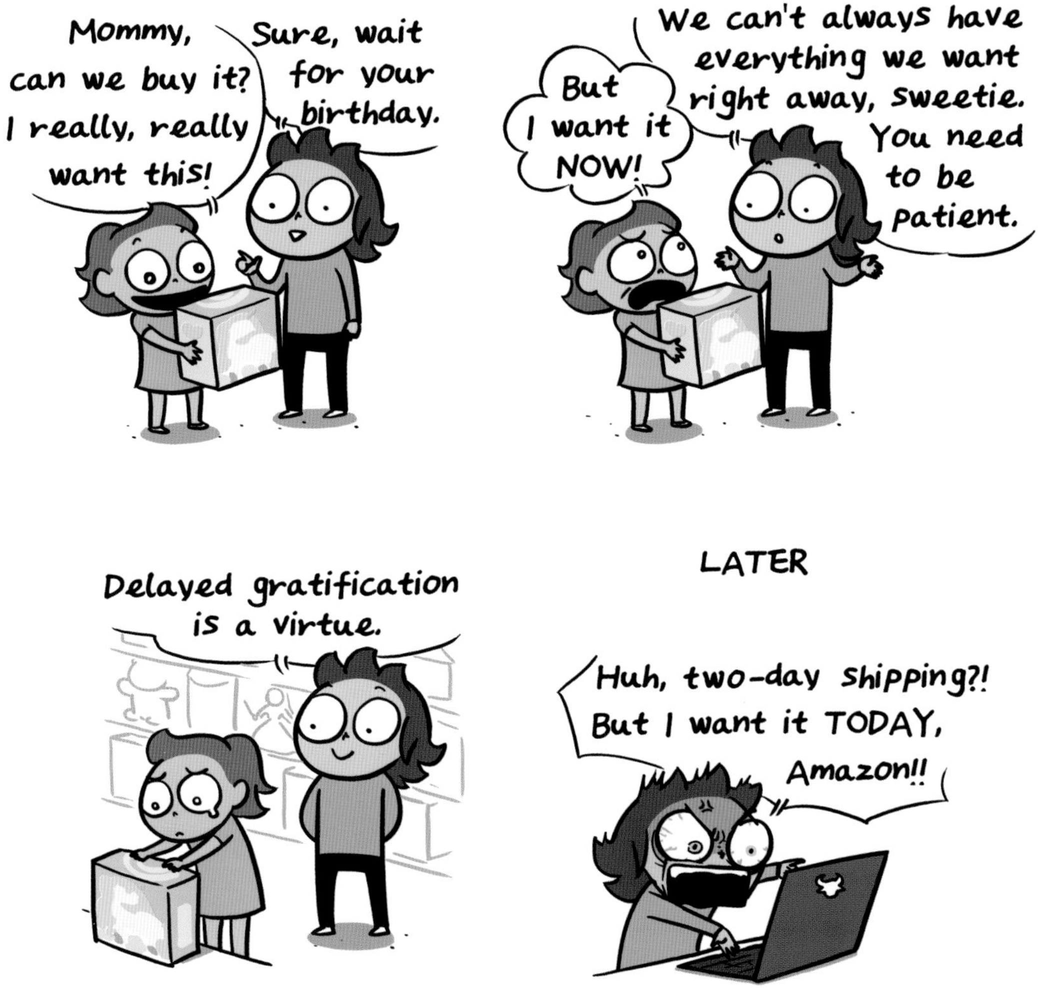
Mommy, can we buy it? I really, really want this!
Sure, wait for your birthday.
But I want it NOW!
We can't always have everything we want right away, sweetie. You need to be patient.
Delayed gratification is a virtue.
LATER
Huh, two-day shipping?! But I want it TODAY, Amazon!!

BELLY RUBS

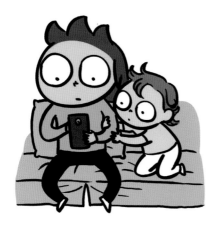

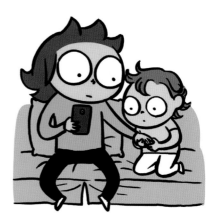

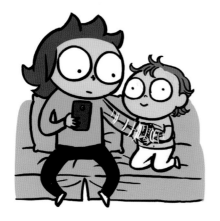

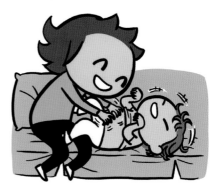

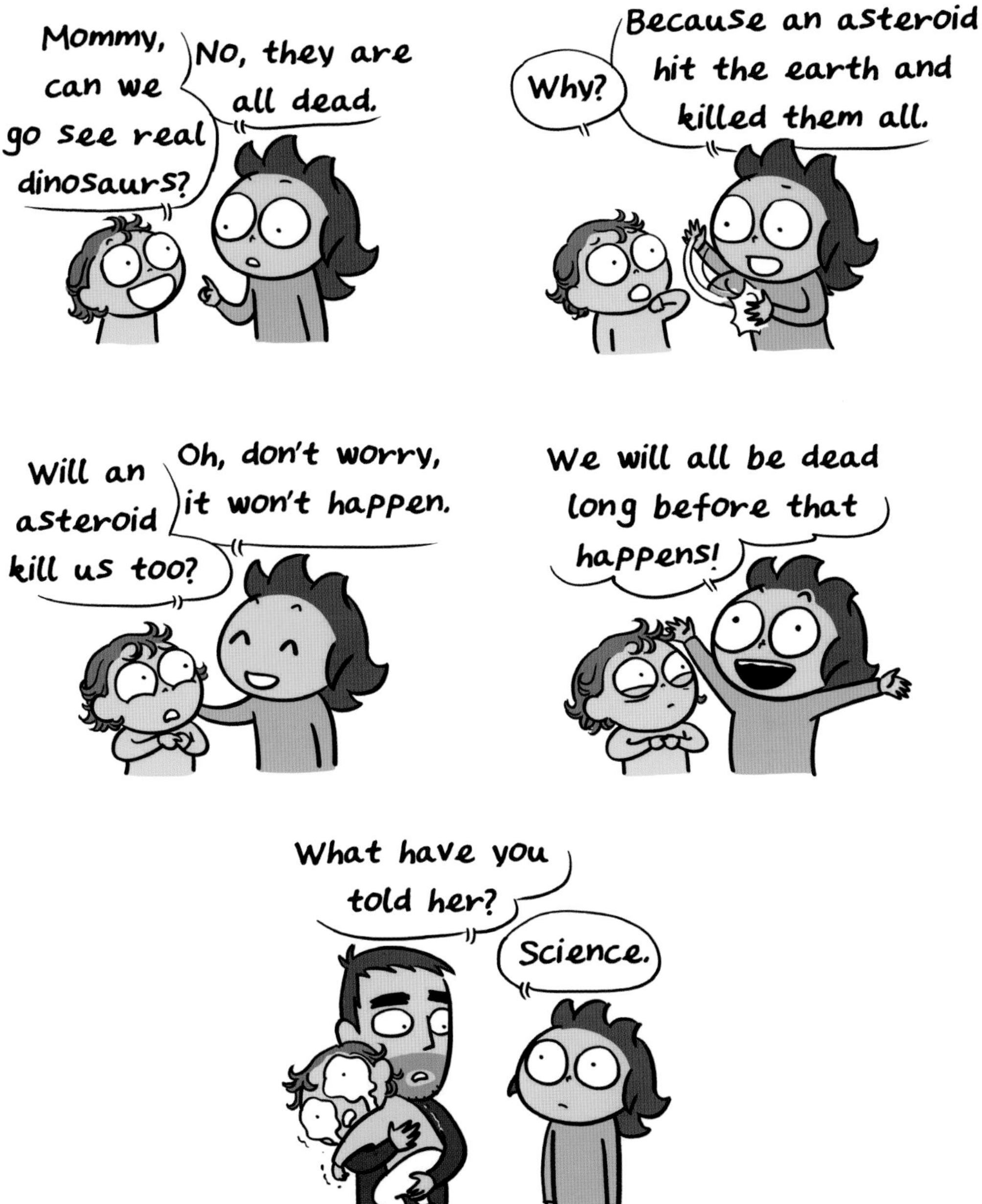
Mommy, can we go see real dinosaurs?
No, they are all dead.
Why?
Because an asteroid hit the earth and killed them all.
Will an asteroid kill us too?
Oh, don't worry, it won't happen.
We will all be dead long before that happens!
What have you told her?
Science.

SUNGLASSES

SOCKS

MY CHILD WEARS
SUNGLASSES

MY CHILD PUTS
ON SOCKS

A BOWL

A TIARA

MY CHILD
USES A BOWL

MY CHILD PUTS
ON A TIARA

A JACKET

MY CHILD
WEARS A JACKET

A CHAIR

MY CHILD SITS
ON A CHAIR

SHOES

MY CHILD
WEARS SHOES

A BED

MY CHILD SLEEPS
IN A BED

STAYING HOME AND WATCHING TV ON SATURDAY NIGHT

BEFORE KIDS

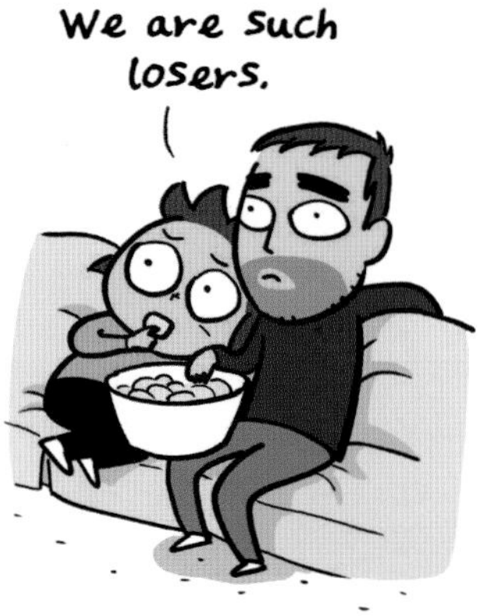
We are such losers.

AFTER KIDS

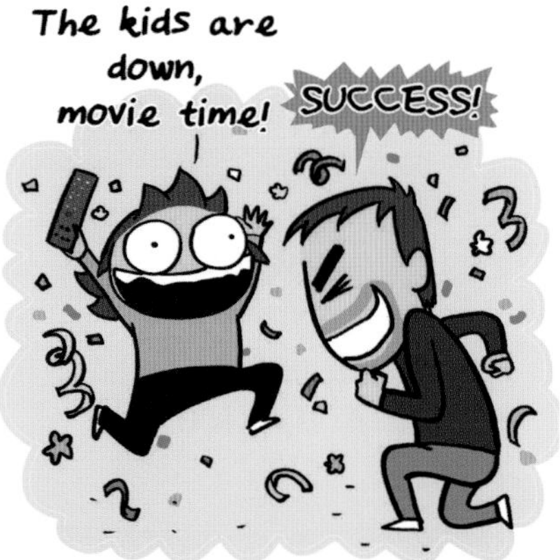
The kids are down, movie time!
SUCCESS!

SHOPPING MALLS

MAGICAL PLACES WHERE I HAD FUN BY SPENDING MONEY AND GETTING PRETTY

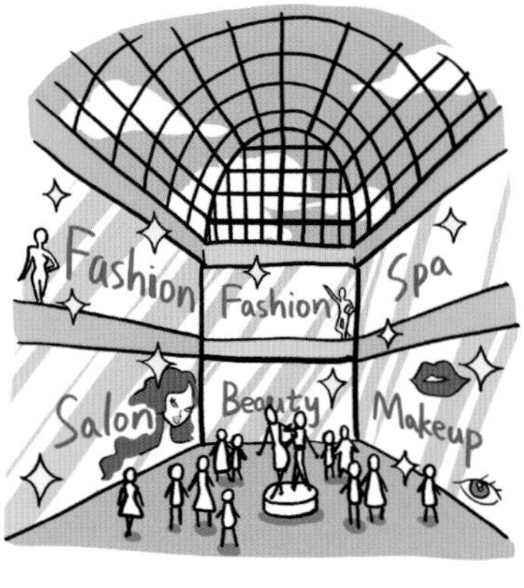
Fashion
Fashion
Spa
Salon
Beauty
Makeup

PUBLIC UTILITIES THAT PROVIDE FOOD, SHELTER, DISTRACTIONS FOR CHILDREN, AND HUMAN CONTACT

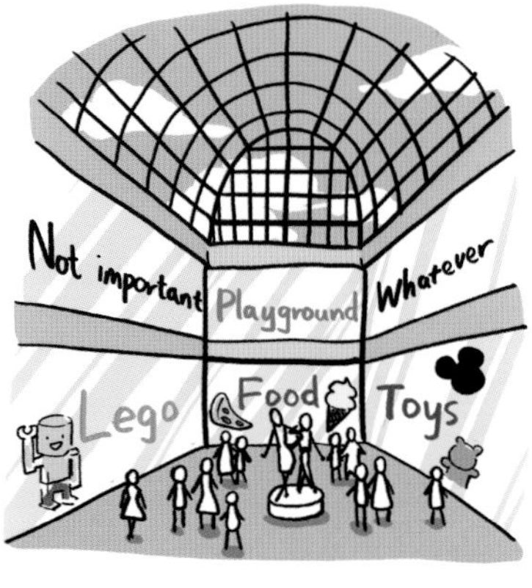
Not important
Playground
Whatever
Lego
Food
Toys

THE WORKPLACE ON MONDAY

BEFORE KIDS

A SUFFOCATING,
LIFE-DRAINING PRISON

AFTER KIDS

A PEACEFUL LAND OF FREEDOM

THE PLAYGROUND

COLORFUL STRUCTURES
SCATTERED IN THE OPEN
AREAS I DROVE BY

WARM AND FRIENDLY FACILITIES
THAT SAVE MY TIRED AND
DESPERATE @#* AND GIVE
ME HOPE AND COURAGE TO LIVE

BEFORE KIDS

NOSTALGIA

AFTER KIDS

A WHIRLPOOL THAT SUCKS
IN YOUR CHILDREN AND MONEY

DINNER

THE MOST RELAXING
TIME OF THE DAY

A MEAL I CAN ONLY
HAVE STANDING UP

Who needs a
dining table?

Here is your
milk, anything
else?

You always
drink it cold.

But I want
it warm!

Hey, that's
my cup!

Can I have
some
candy?

WEEKENDS

BEFORE KIDS

THE SLEEPY AND SLOW

AFTER KIDS

THE FAST AND THE FURIOUS

VACATIONS

BEING SOMEWHERE FAR AWAY AND BEAUTIFUL

ALONE TIME IN THE BATHROOM OF MY OWN HOUSE

CARDBOARD BOXES

BEFORE KIDS

TRASH THAT TAKES
A LOT OF SPACE

AFTER KIDS

BUILDING BLOCKS OF
ENDLESS FUN

PET CATS

MY BABIES, MY FAMILY,
THE FOCUS OF MY CAMERA,
THE CUTEST CREATURES
IN THE WORLD

ORDINARY HOUSE ANIMALS
THAT REQUIRE LITTLE
WORK TO KEEP ALIVE, AND
PLAYMATES FOR THE KIDS

WEARING RELAXED SPORTSWEAR

A messy and unorganized mom

WEARING TIGHT SPORTSWEAR

An active and energetic mom

THE BEGINNING OF SUMMER

Let's pick out the best summer camps! Art, dance, sports ...oh and STEM! You will have such a fun and productive summer!

ONE MONTH INTO SUMMER

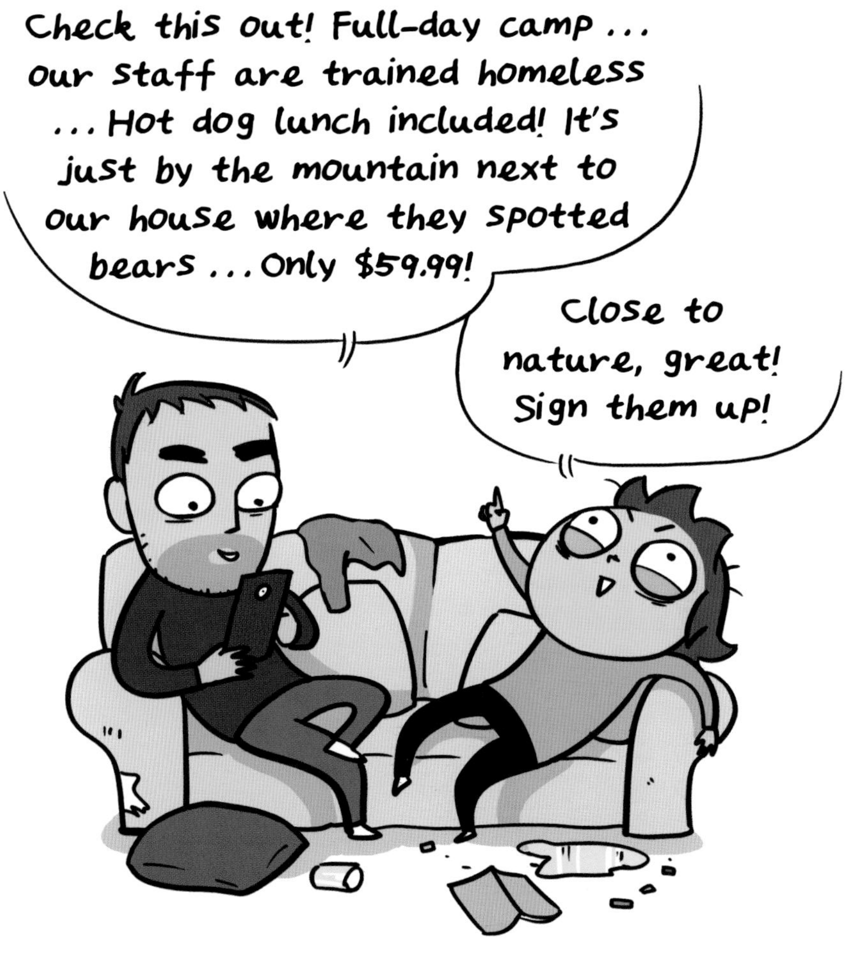
Check this out! Full-day camp ... our staff are trained homeless ... Hot dog lunch included! It's just by the mountain next to our house where they spotted bears ... Only $59.99!
Close to nature, great! Sign them up!

STUDENTS

THE FIRST DAY OF KINDERGARTEN

THE FIRST DAY OF ALL THE OTHER GRADES

PARENTS

THE FIRST DAY OF KINDERGARTEN

THE FIRST DAY OF ALL THE OTHER GRADES

TEACHERS

THE FIRST DAY OF KINDERGARTEN

THE FIRST DAY OF ALL THE OTHER GRADES

Bye! Have fun at school!

Peace! Space! Freedom! Energy! You give me so much. Thank you, School!

You are welcome.

Germs from School?

It's too generous.

WHEN MY HUSBAND GETS A HAIRCUT

OMG! Who is this handsome stranger in my house?

WHEN I GET A HAIRCUT

THREE DAYS LATER

Did you notice that I cut my hair?

Y-yeah. I was thinking you looked different today!

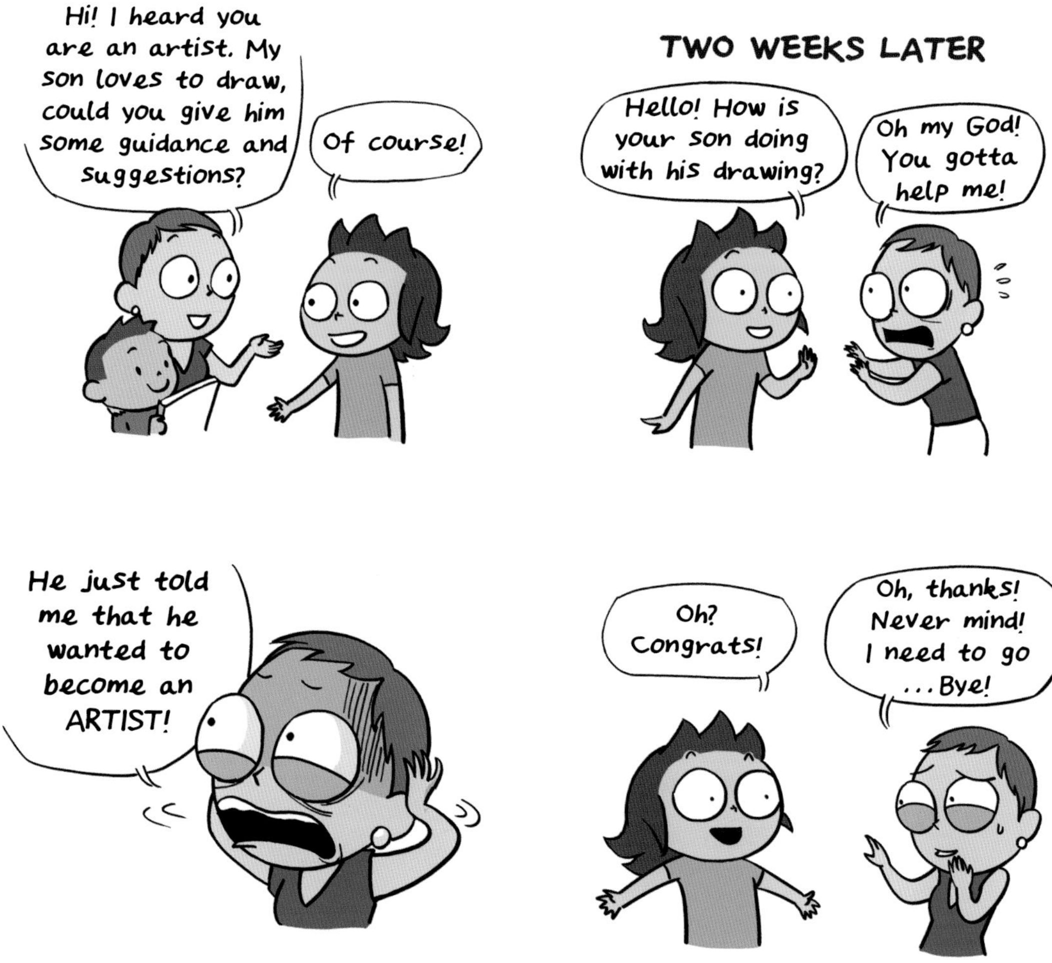
Hi! I heard you are an artist. My son loves to draw, could you give him some guidance and suggestions?
Of course!
TWO WEEKS LATER
Hello! How is your son doing with his drawing?
Oh my God! You gotta help me!
He just told me that he wanted to become an ARTIST!
Oh? Congrats!
Oh, thanks! Never mind! I need to go ...Bye!

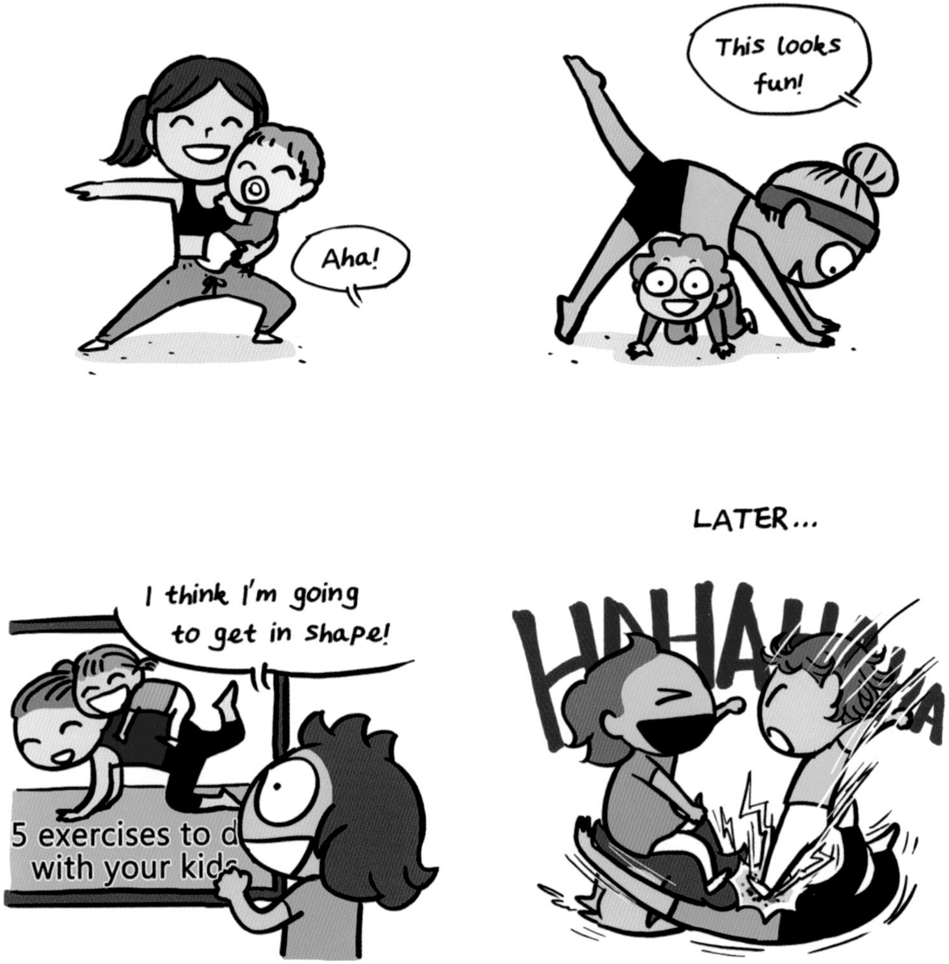
Aha!
This looks fun!
I think I'm going to get in shape!
5 exercises to d
with your kids
LATER...

PACKING FOR VACATION

ME WHEN I WAS YOUNG

DIFFERENT COMBINATIONS EVERY DAY

+ Accessories + Makeup + Lotion & Cream

Do you need so much stuff?

You don't understand.

ME NOW

MY KIDS' STUFF

MY STUFF

One pair of fresh jeans and one pair of comfortable shoes,

and a warm jacket just in case. Done!

TAKING PICTURES ON VACATION

ME WHEN I WAS YOUNG

ME NOW

SHOPPING FOR CLOTHES

ME WHEN I WAS YOUNG

These are a bit tight,
but they will fit after
I lose some weight.

ME NOW

They fit just right.
I need a bigger size in
case I get fat.

ACHIEVEMENTS

ME WHEN I WAS YOUNG

There are so many things
you can do!
How can you call it an
achievement to just have KIDS?

ME NOW

My biggest achievement
in my life is my FAMILY.

MUSIC

ME WHEN I WAS YOUNG

This is the new album by
(underground band name),
have you listened?
It's dope.

Yeah!
I love them!

Never heard
of them

It's not quite pleasant...
No wait! I NEED to listen
to it, it's the @#$%!

ME NOW

What? This music video has
been played over 10 million
times and I've never heard of
it. Maybe I should check it out.

Old
songs
I always
listen to

Nah,
why do I care.

LATE NIGHT

ME WHEN I WAS YOUNG

This show is good. I'm gonna binge-watch it all night.

NEXT DAY AFTERNOON

ME NOW

I'm tired. I will just finish this work and go to bed.

EARLY NEXT MORNING

Why do I wake up so early? Why can't I fall back asleep? I want to die...

DREAMS

CHILDHOOD

I want to be a Scientist
or an astronaut!

You have your entire
life ahead of you,
just study hard and
your dreams will
come true!

TEENAGE

I want to be a singer!
An artist is not bad either.

Just work
toward your
dreams,
everything is
possible!

YOUNG ADULT

I could be like
them if I spent
some time ...

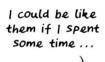

Elites and Celebrities

Then do it!
It takes a lot of
time and effort, but
you can make it!

NOW

I don't have much time left!

... ...

Thump

73

I wonder what time it is.

Ah . . .

I wonder what time it is.

IT'S AWKWARD AND SAD TO
HAVE A REAL MEAL ALONE.

BUT PERFECTLY NORMAL
FOR THE SNACKS.

WEAPON: HEAD

SCENE 1

the front tooth

BANG!

suddenly!

Target: Chin

Damage: ★ ★ ★

SCENE 2

Daddy!

Target: Crotch

Damage: ★ ★ ★ ★ (to moms)

∞ (to dads)

WEAPON: BUTT

SCENE 1

Target: Back
Damage: ⭐⭐⭐

SCENE 2

Target: Belly
Damage: ⭐⭐⭐⭐

WEAPON: WEIGHT

Target: Whole Body

Damage: ★ ★ ★ ★ ★

WEAPON: FEET

SCENE 1

Target: Face
Damage: ★ ★ ★ ★

SCENE 2

Target: Crotch
Damage: ★ ★ ★ ★ ★ (to dads)

SCENE 3

Look at what Mommy bought you!

Wow, heels!

Target: Feet
Damage: ★ ★ ★ ★

WEAPON: GAS

SCENE 1

Ppprrt
tt...

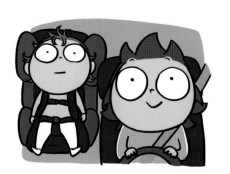

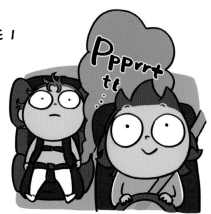

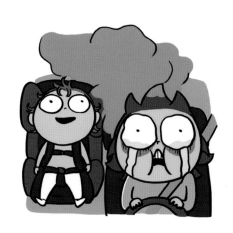

SCENE 2

My face smells
like @#$%.

Target: Respiratory System
Your Pride

Damage: ★★★★★

WEAPON: HANDS

SCENE 1

Who is a cute baby?
You are a cute ba...

...by

WHACK!

Target: Face
Damage: ★ ★ ★
+ $ for glasses

SCENE 2

Hmmm...

Mommy,
get up.

......

Mommy,
get up!

Target: Nostrils
Damage: ★ ★ ★ ★

SCENE 3

Just spent 20 minutes
doing my hair, I'm
feeling pretty!

Hey, don't
mess with
my hair!

Hahaha!

Target: Hair

Damage: ★ ★ ★ ★ ★

WEAPON: VOICE

SCENE 1

Lasting over 10 minutes . . .

SCENE 2

Mommy, are
we there?

Not yet.

When will we
be there?

About 20
minutes.

ONE MINUTE LATER

Are we there?

No, not so fast.

TEN SECONDS LATER

Why aren't
we there?

Because!

Are we there? Are we there?
We are still not there? Mom?
Are we there? Why aren't we
there? Mom? Are we
there? Are we there? Mom?
Are we...

SCENE 3

HAPPY

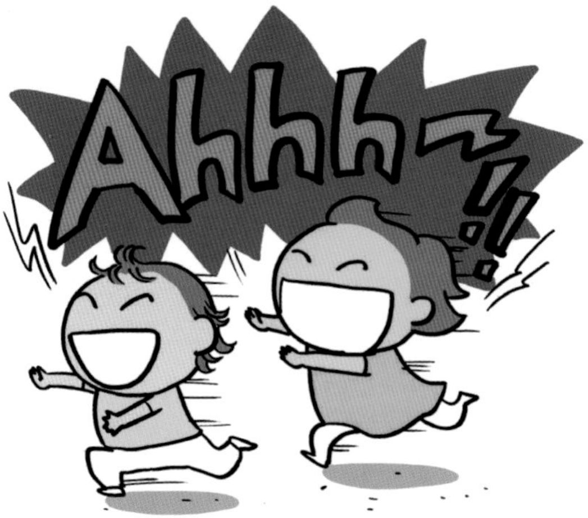
Ahhh~!!

SAD

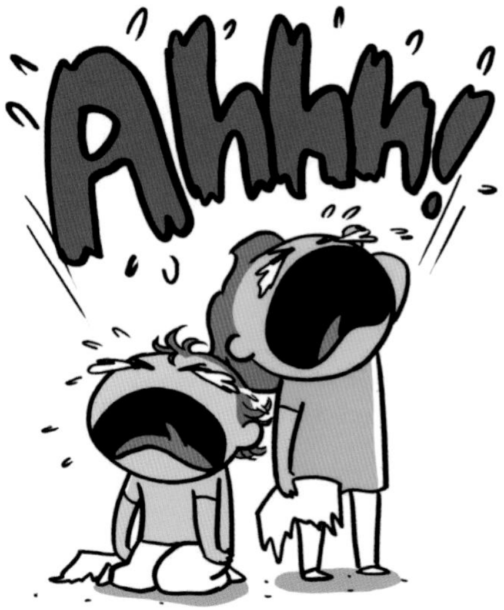
Ahhh!

ANGRY

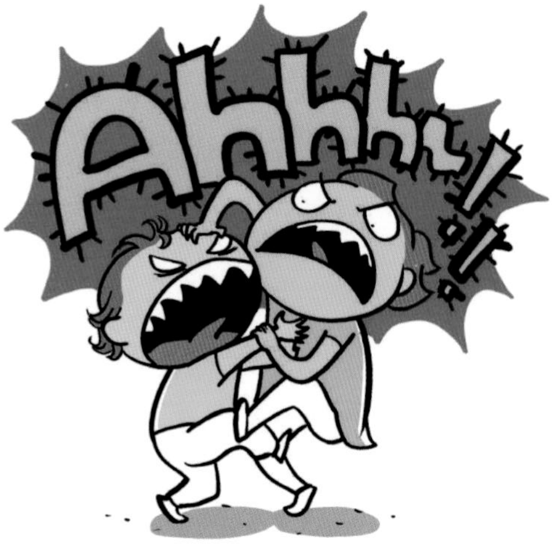
Ahhh!!

BORED

Target: Your Eardrums
        Your Patience
        and Your Sanity

Damage: ★★★★★

WEAPON: POOP

Target: Respiratory System

Damage: ★★★★

88

THE ULTIMATE WEAPON

Why do I do this
to myself?

I'm in such pain,
and it's all
because of YOU!

I will stay away
from you,
for my health.

Mommy?

Play horse with me,
please?

CUTENESS!

HAHAHAHA!!

This is my life now.

Target: Your Soul
Damage: ★★★★

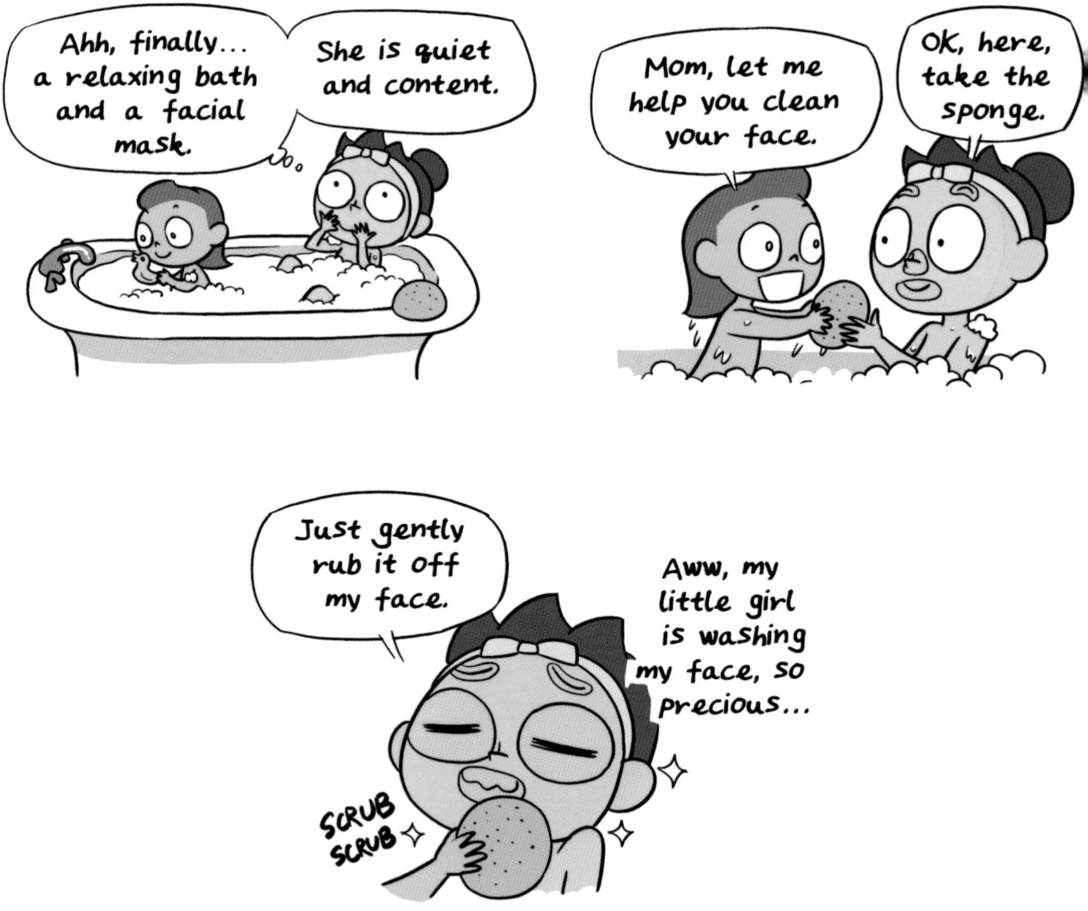
Ahh, finally... a relaxing bath and a facial mask.
She is quiet and content.
Mom, let me help you clean your face.
OK, here, take the sponge.
Just gently rub it off my face.
Aww, my little girl is washing my face, so precious...
SCRUB SCRUB

The
reward
of being
a mom...

Hello? Can
you keep...

SCRUB
SCRUB

LUNCH IN A SANDWICH BAG

A NORMAL MOM

LUNCH IN A SANDWICH BAG WITH DRAWINGS ON IT

AN AWESOME MOM

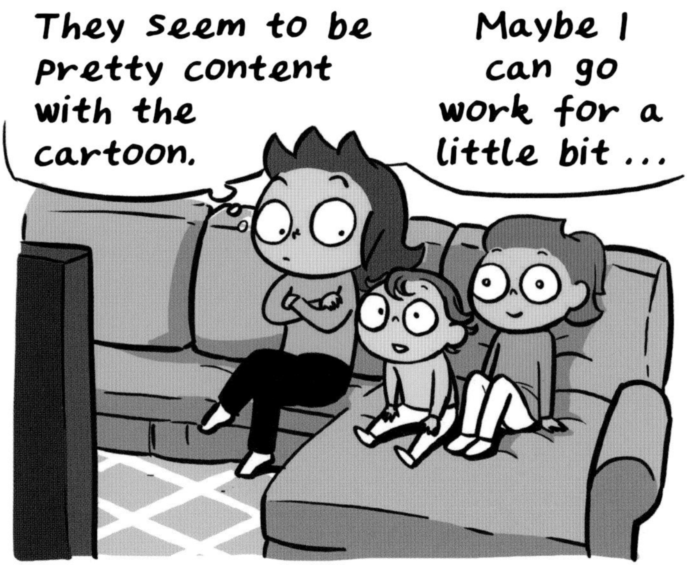
They seem to be pretty content with the cartoon.
Maybe I can go work for a little bit ...

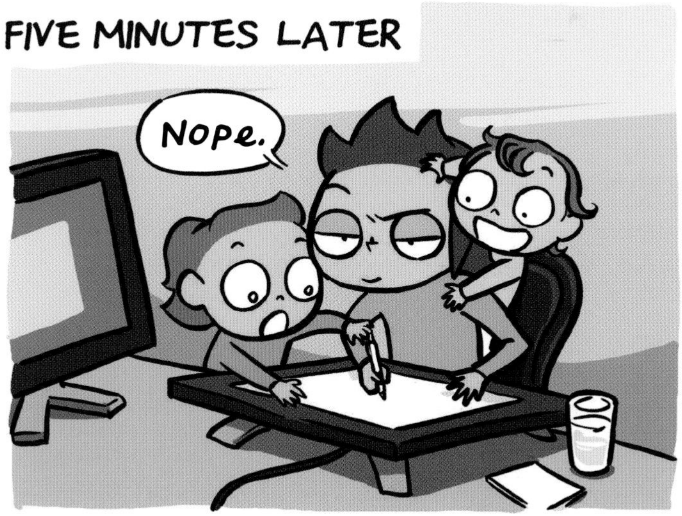
FIVE MINUTES LATER
Nope.

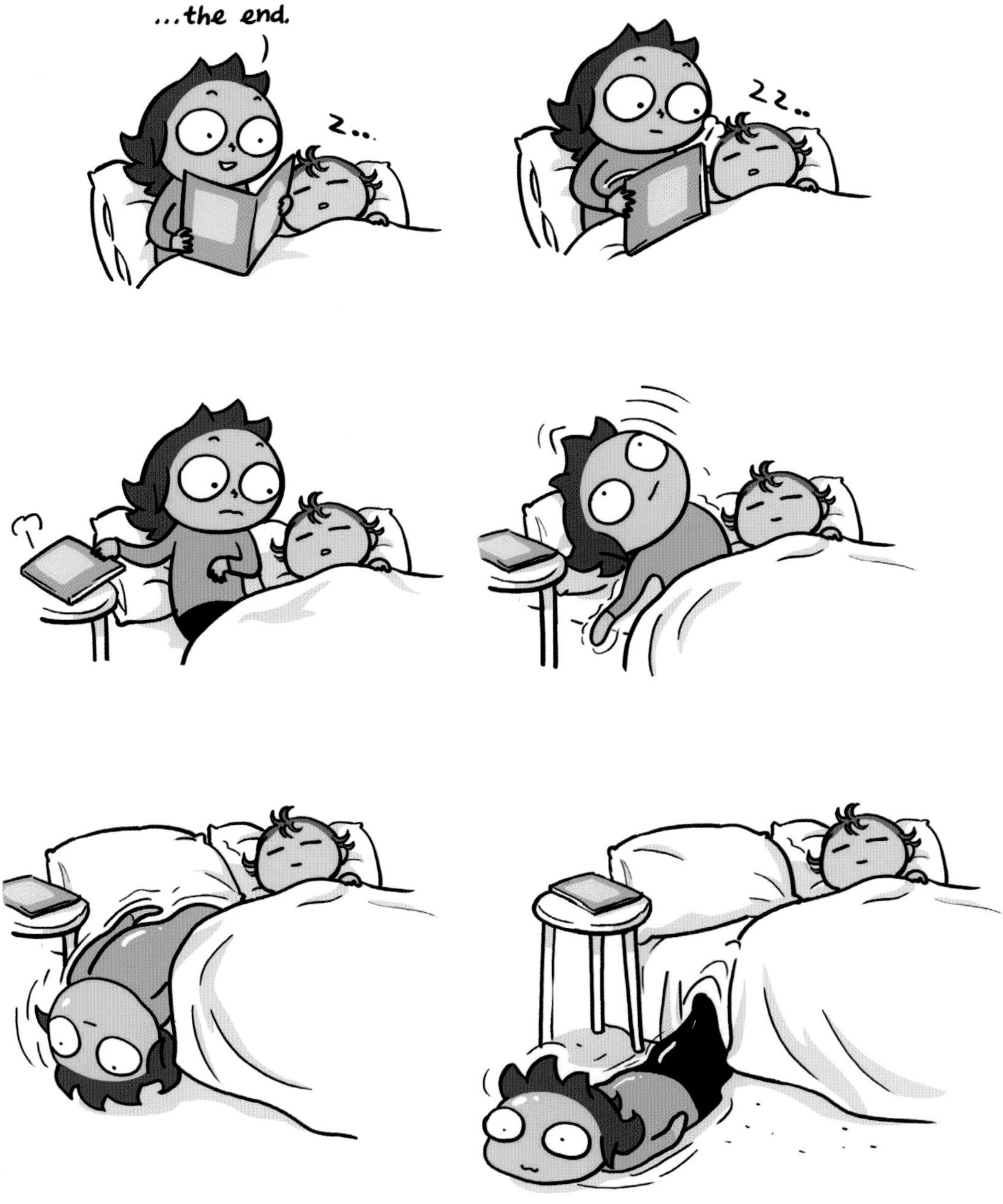
...the end.
z...
zz...

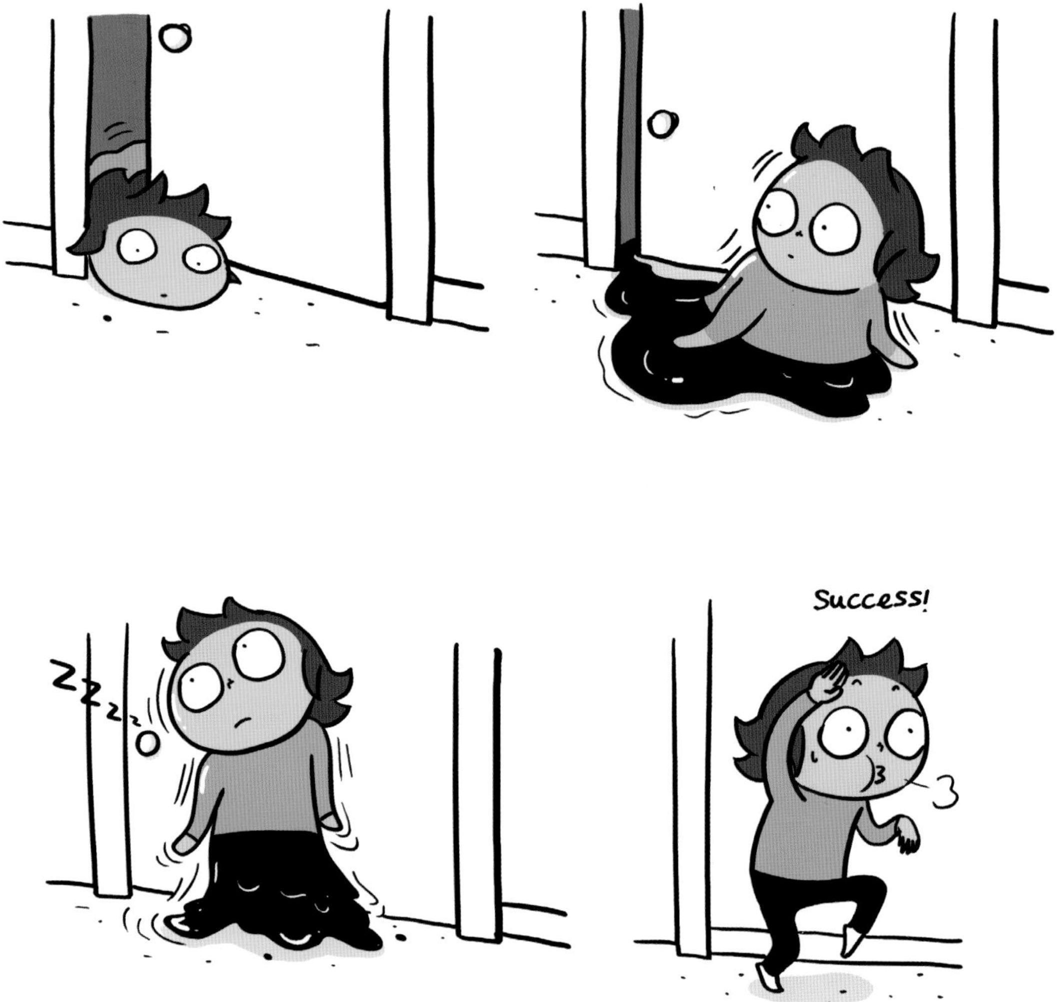
ZZzz
SUCCESS!

HOW TO GET
EVERYONE'S ATTENTION IN MY HOUSE

HUSBAND

Dinner is ready!   ......   I'm naked!

Yes?

MOM

Hmm, I need help...   WHAT CAN I DO FOR YOU, HONEY?!

8:30 PM

Bi bi bi bi

It's time!

Inhale

Kids!
Time to
go to bed!

Hurry up!
Mommy needs to
draw an epic comic
after you sleep!

8:45 PM

Control my temper,
be gentle and
patient, they will
listen to reason.

Breathe
deeply

OK!
Jumping time is over,
get to sleep!

If you keep playing,
you can't get up in
time and will be late
for school!

Smiling

Boing   Boing   Boing

8:55 PM

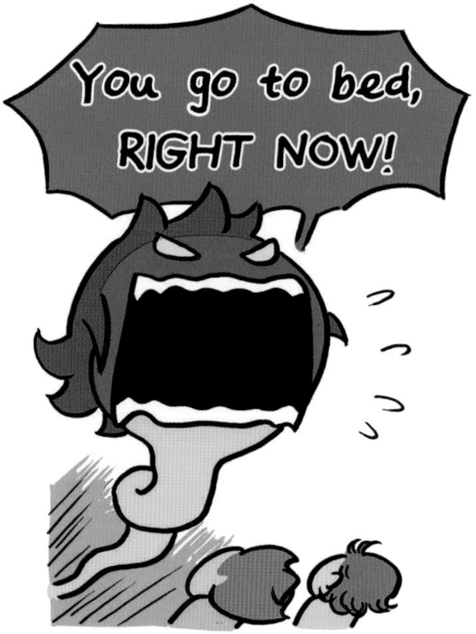
You go to bed,
RIGHT NOW!

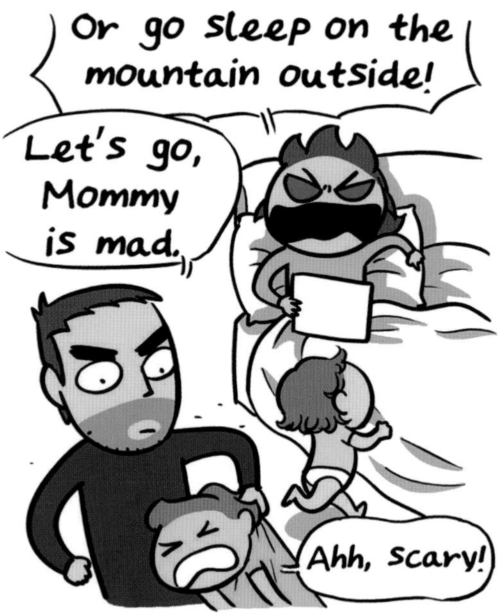
Or go sleep on the mountain outside!
Let's go, Mommy is mad.
Ahh, scary!

9:00 PM

I'm sorry, I shouldn't have yelled at you. Calm down, calm down! I'm a good mom!

Come on, sweetie. How many stories do you want tonight?

OK. We will go to sleep after three stories.

9:15 PM

Warm and lovely
mother-child time

9:30 PM

Finished,
let's sleep!

One
more!

Yes,
sleep,
sleep.

9:32 PM

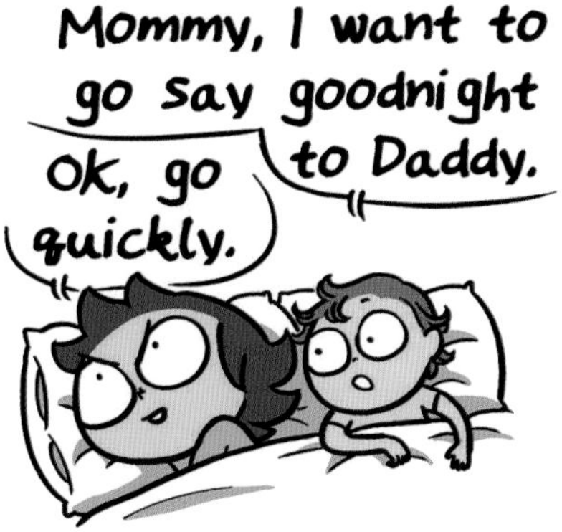
Mommy, I want to go say goodnight to Daddy.
Ok, go quickly.

9:38 PM

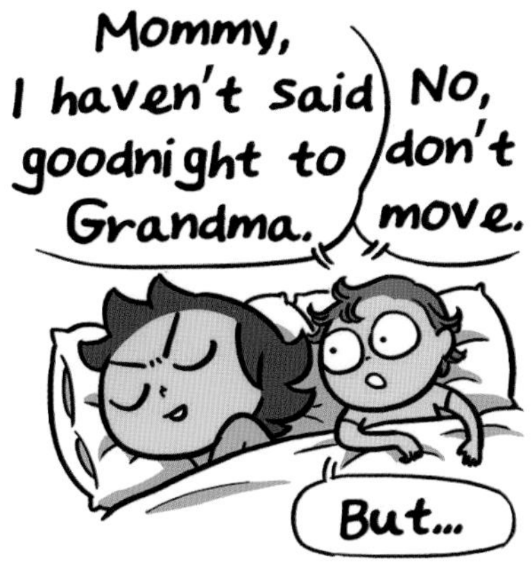
Mommy, I haven't said goodnight to Grandma.
No, don't move.
But...

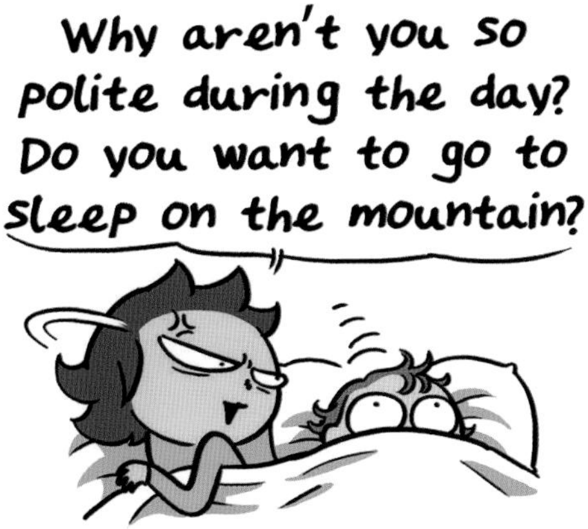
Why aren't you so polite during the day? Do you want to go to sleep on the mountain?

9:43 PM

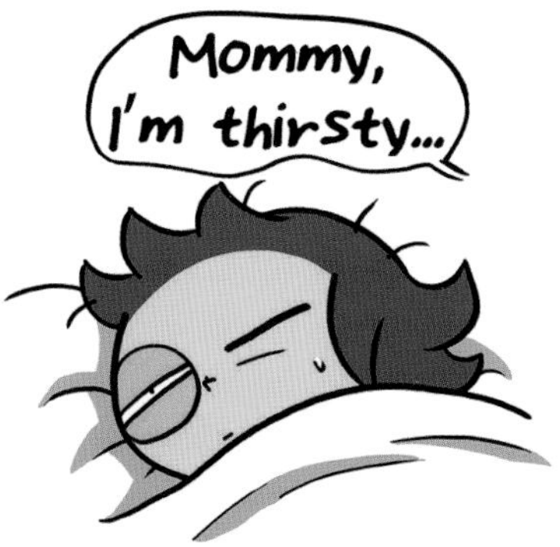
Mommy, I'm thirsty...

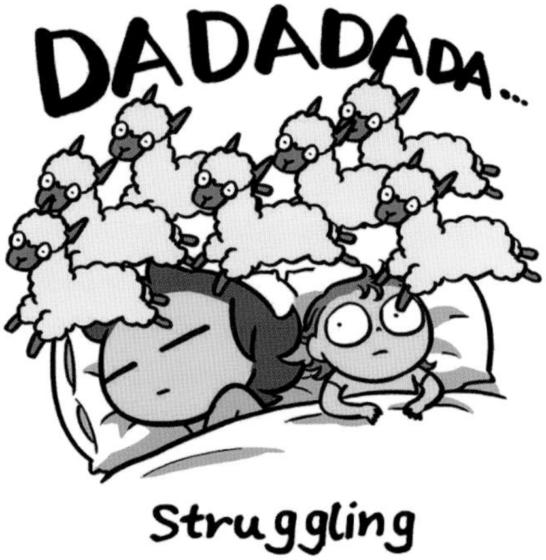
DADADADA...
Struggling

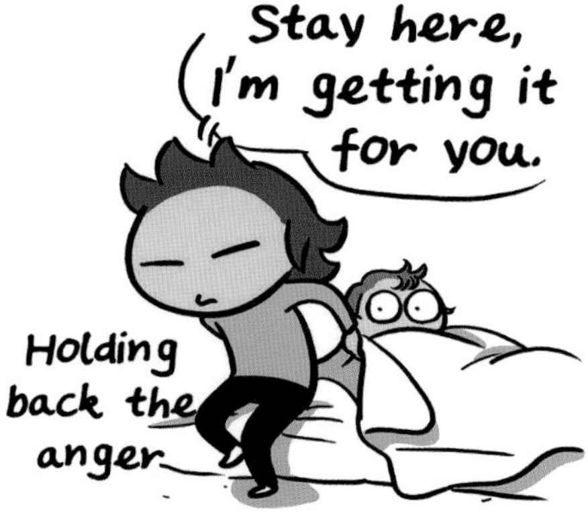
Stay here, I'm getting it for you.
Holding back the anger

9:50 PM

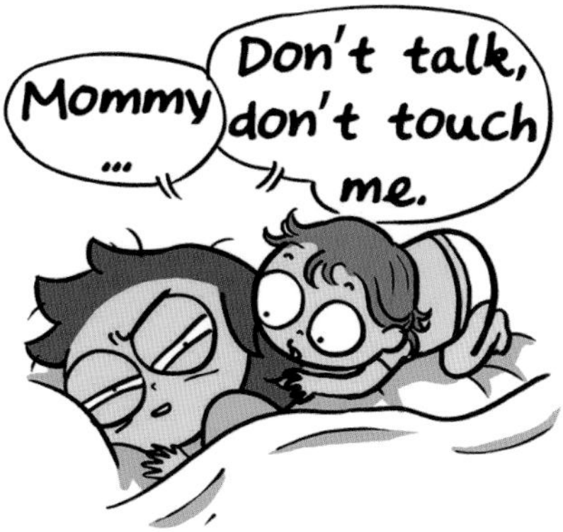
Mommy ...
Don't talk, don't touch me.

9:55 PM

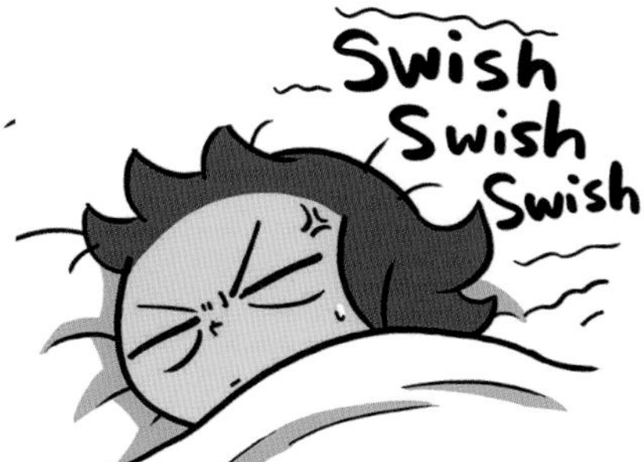
Swish
Swish
Swish

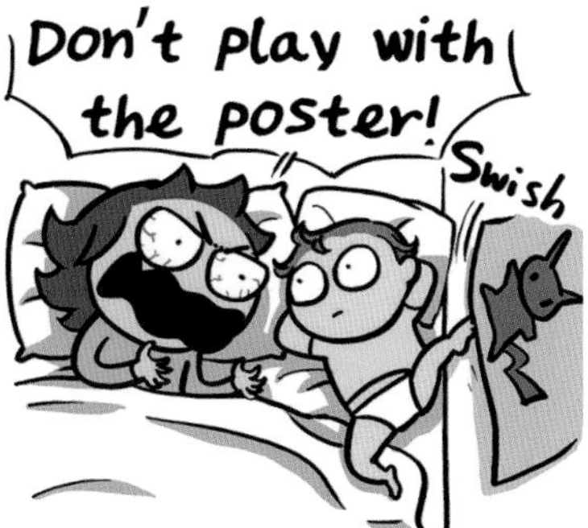
Don't play with the poster!
Swish

Come here, close
your eyes, I will
scratch your back.

10:05 PM

My arm is tired.

I think I can stop.

10:15 PM

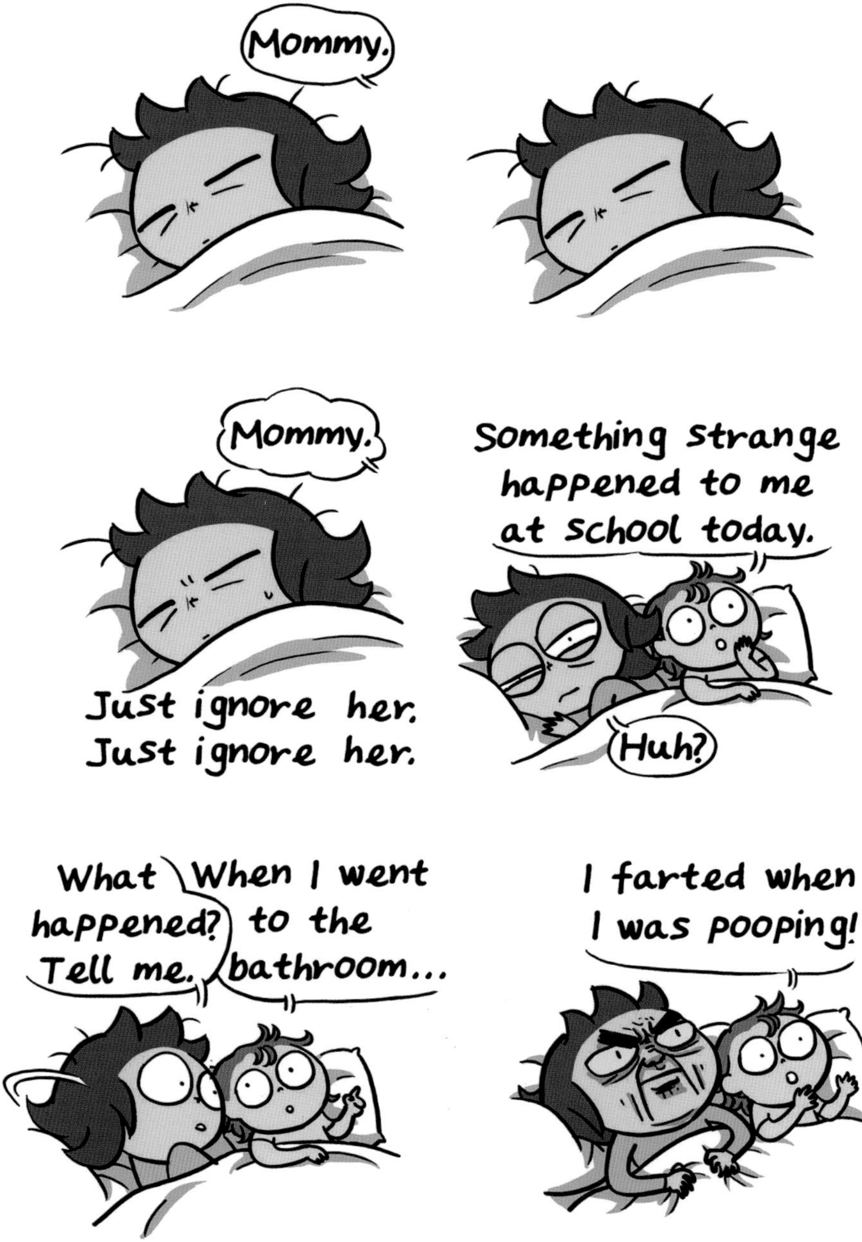
Mommy.
Mommy.
Just ignore her. Just ignore her.
Something strange happened to me at school today.
Huh?
What happened? Tell me.
When I went to the bathroom...
I farted when I was pooping!

10:30 PM

OH, NO.

SORRY, I WAS TOO TIRED
TO TELL REALITY
FROM IMAGINATION.

10:30 PM (for real)

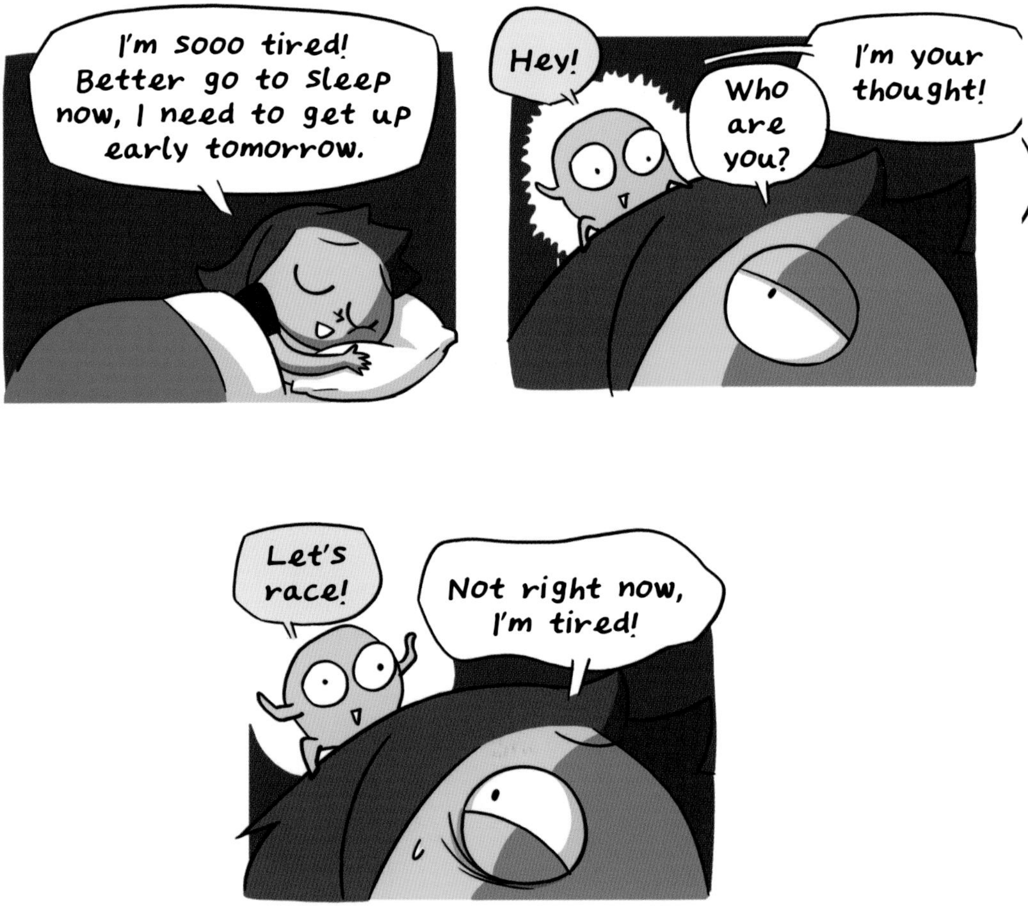
I'm sooo tired! Better go to sleep now, I need to get up early tomorrow.
Hey!
Who are you?
I'm your thought!
Let's race!
Not right now, I'm tired!

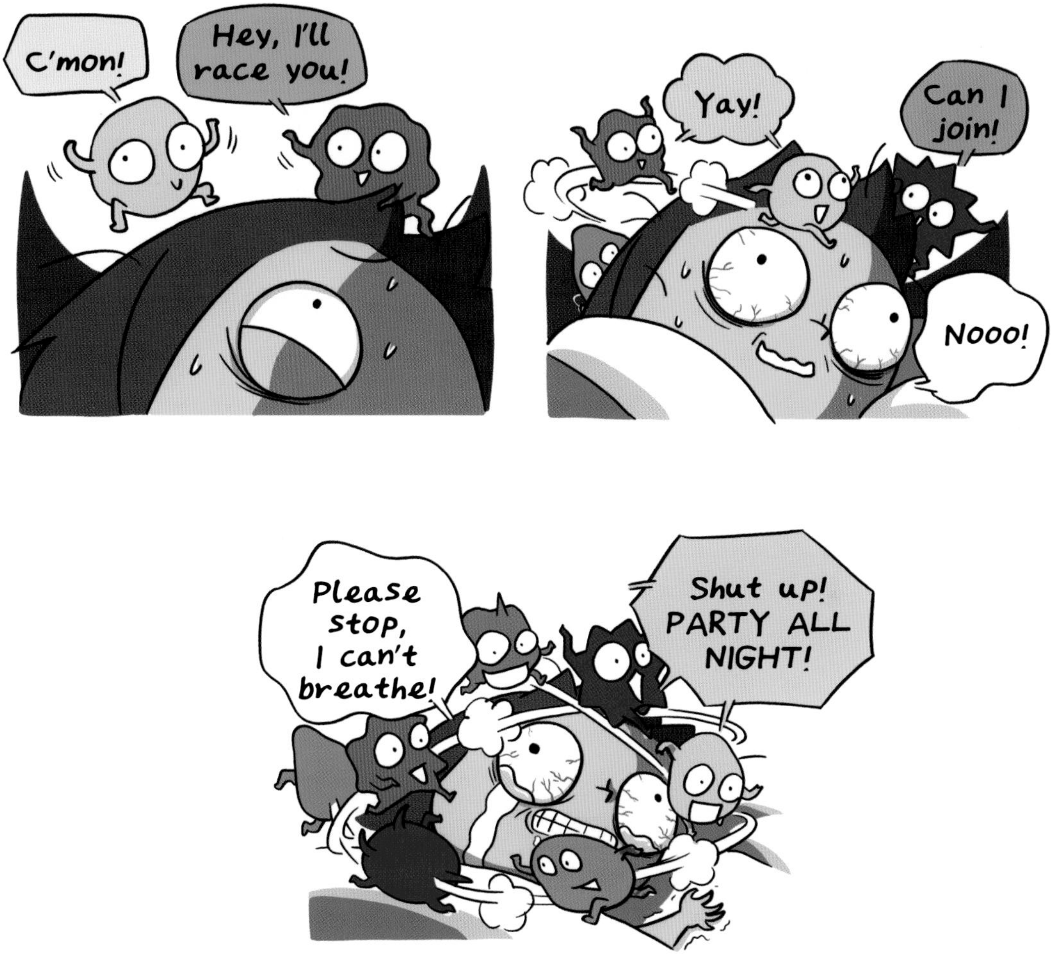
C'mon!
Hey, I'll race you!
Yay!
Can I join!
Nooo!
Please stop, I can't breathe!
Shut up! PARTY ALL NIGHT!

IF MY TWO-YEAR-OLD WAS AN OFFICE WORKER

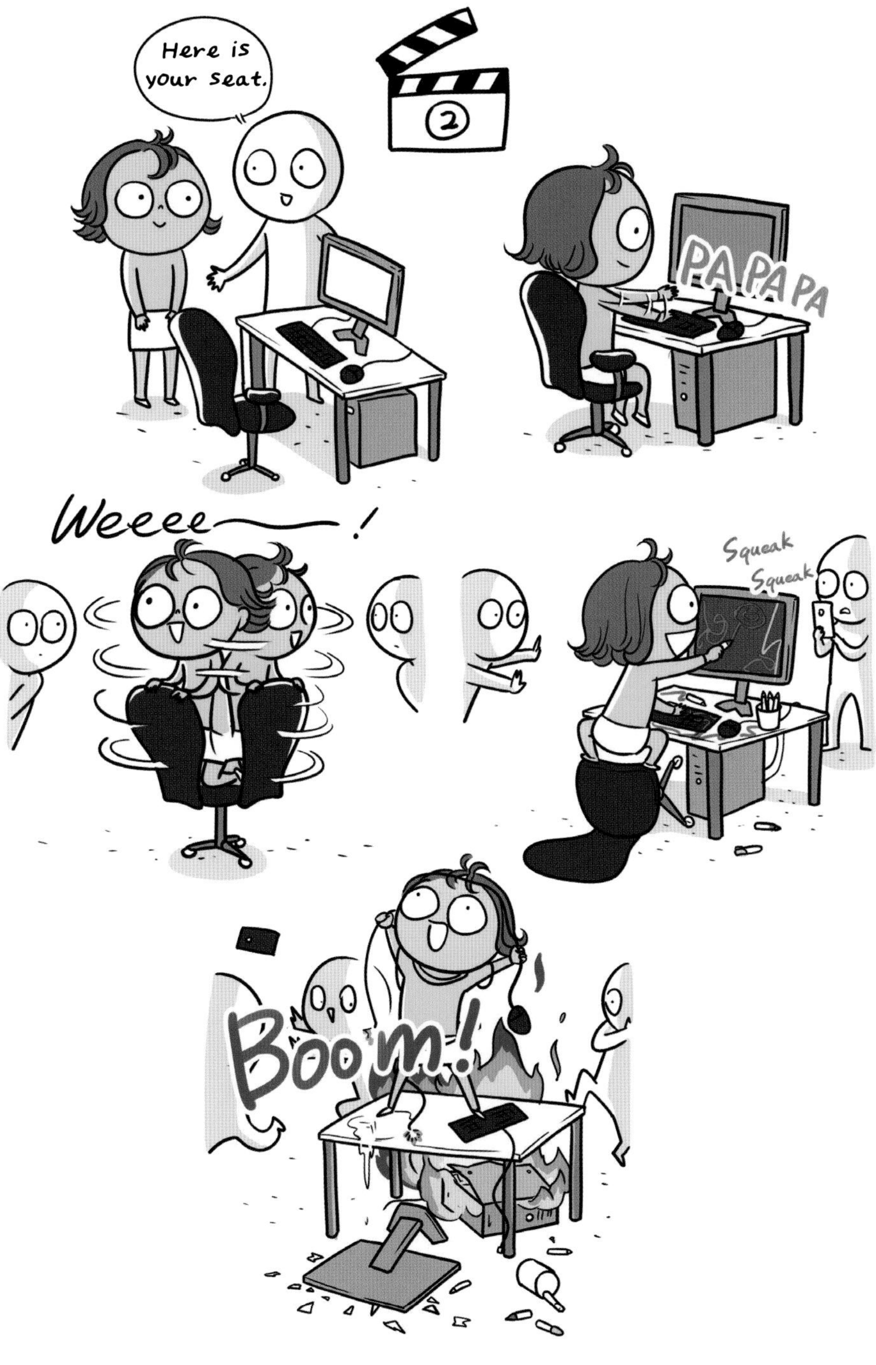

Here is your seat.
2
PA PA PA
Weeee——!
Squeak
Squeak
Boom!

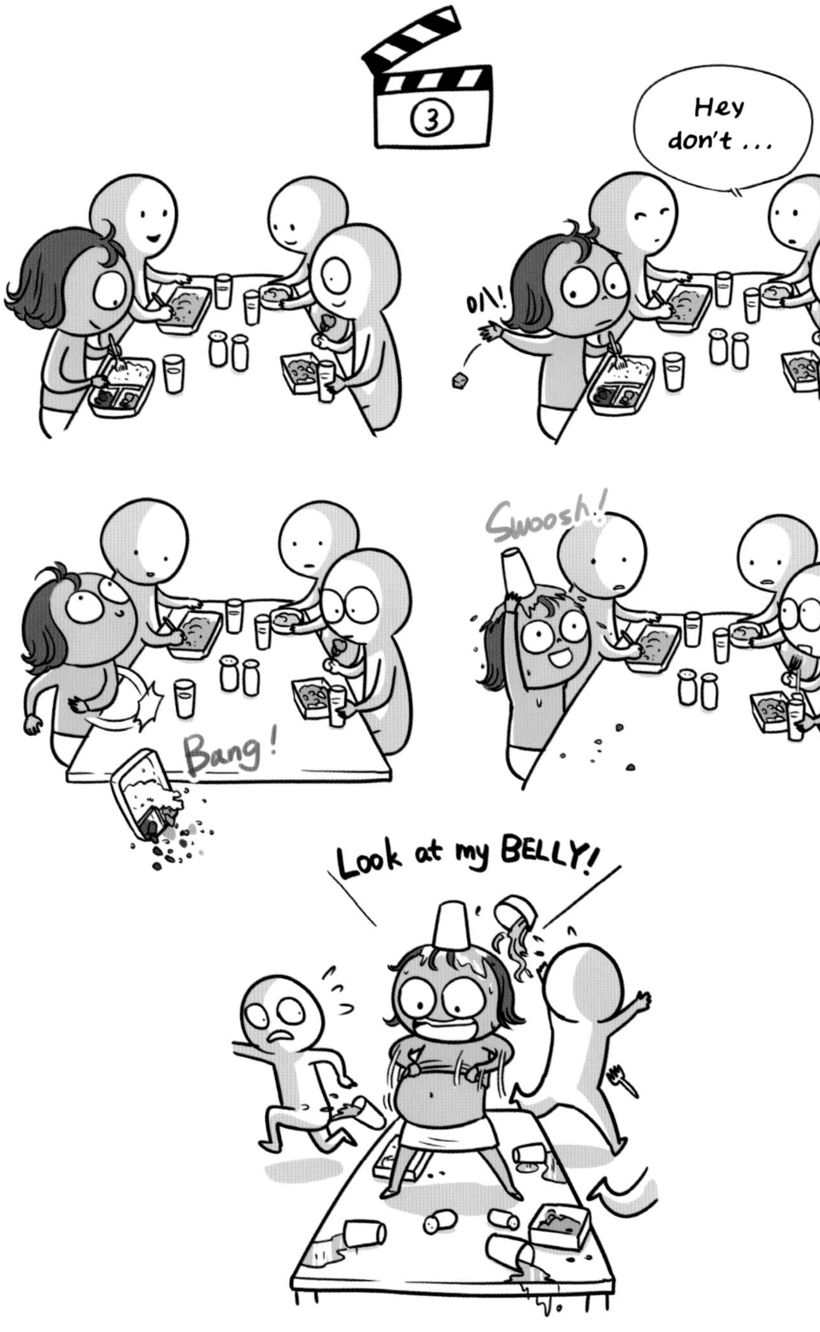
Hey don't ...
Oh!
Bang!
Swoosh!
Look at my BELLY!

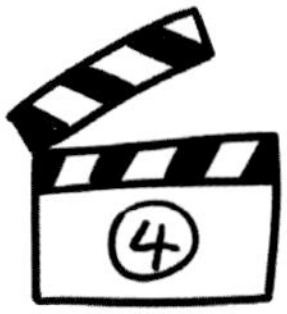
4

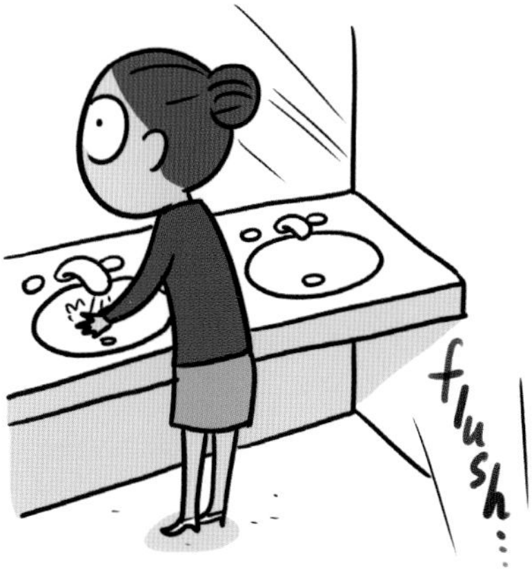
flush...

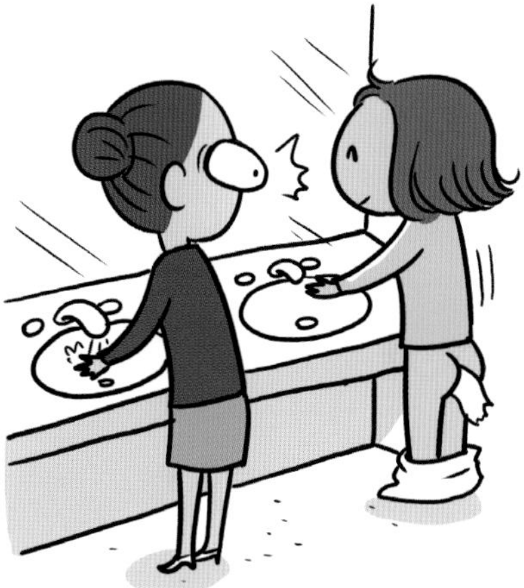

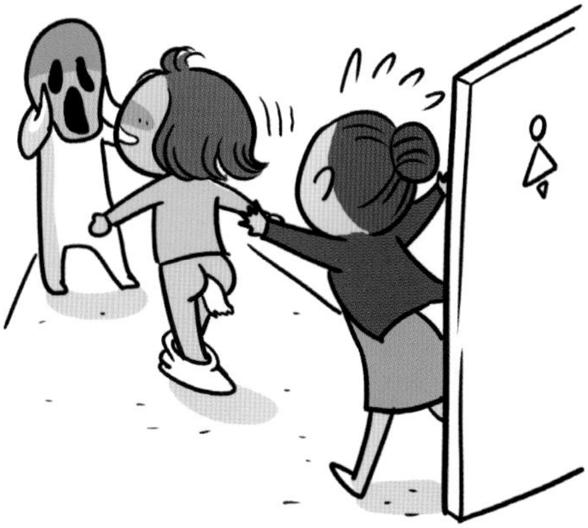

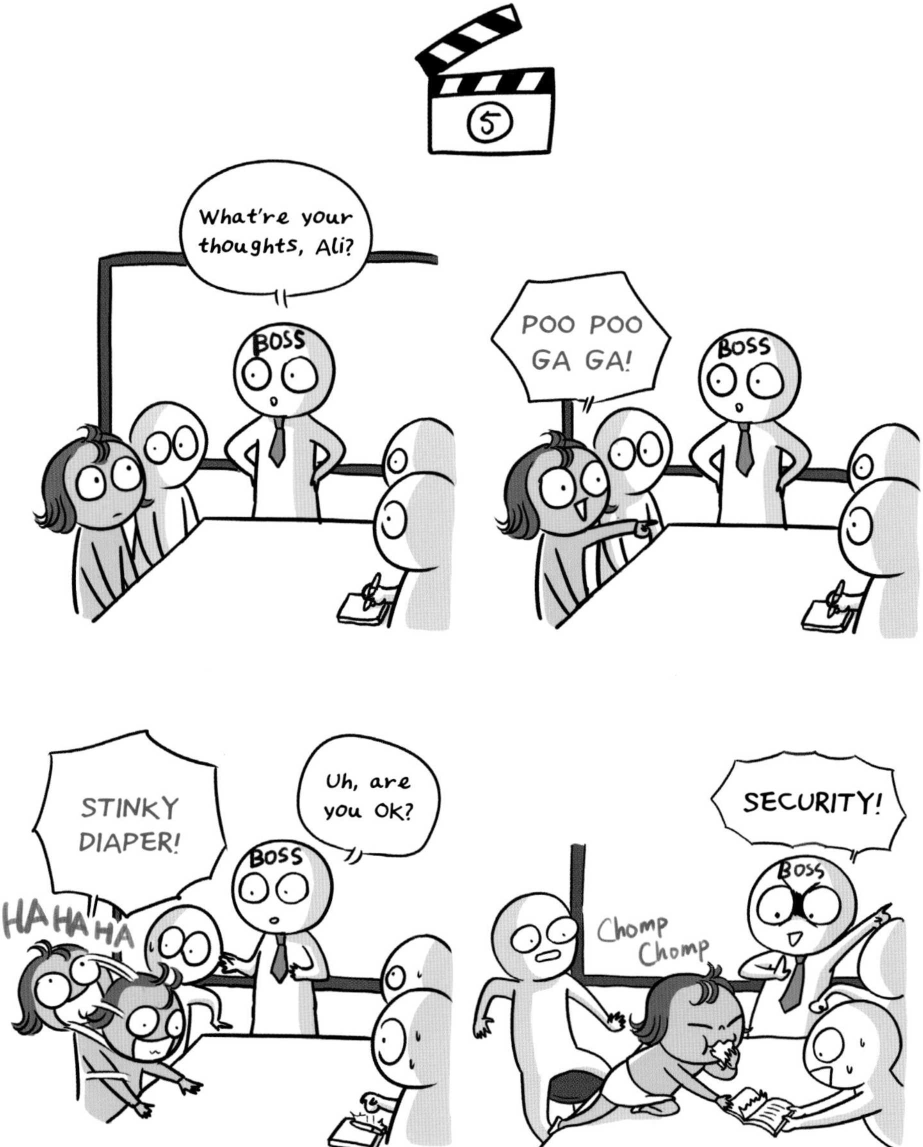
5
What're your thoughts, Ali?
BOSS
POO POO GA GA!
BOSS
STINKY DIAPER!
HA HA HA HA
Uh, are you OK?
BOSS
SECURITY!
BOSS
Chomp Chomp

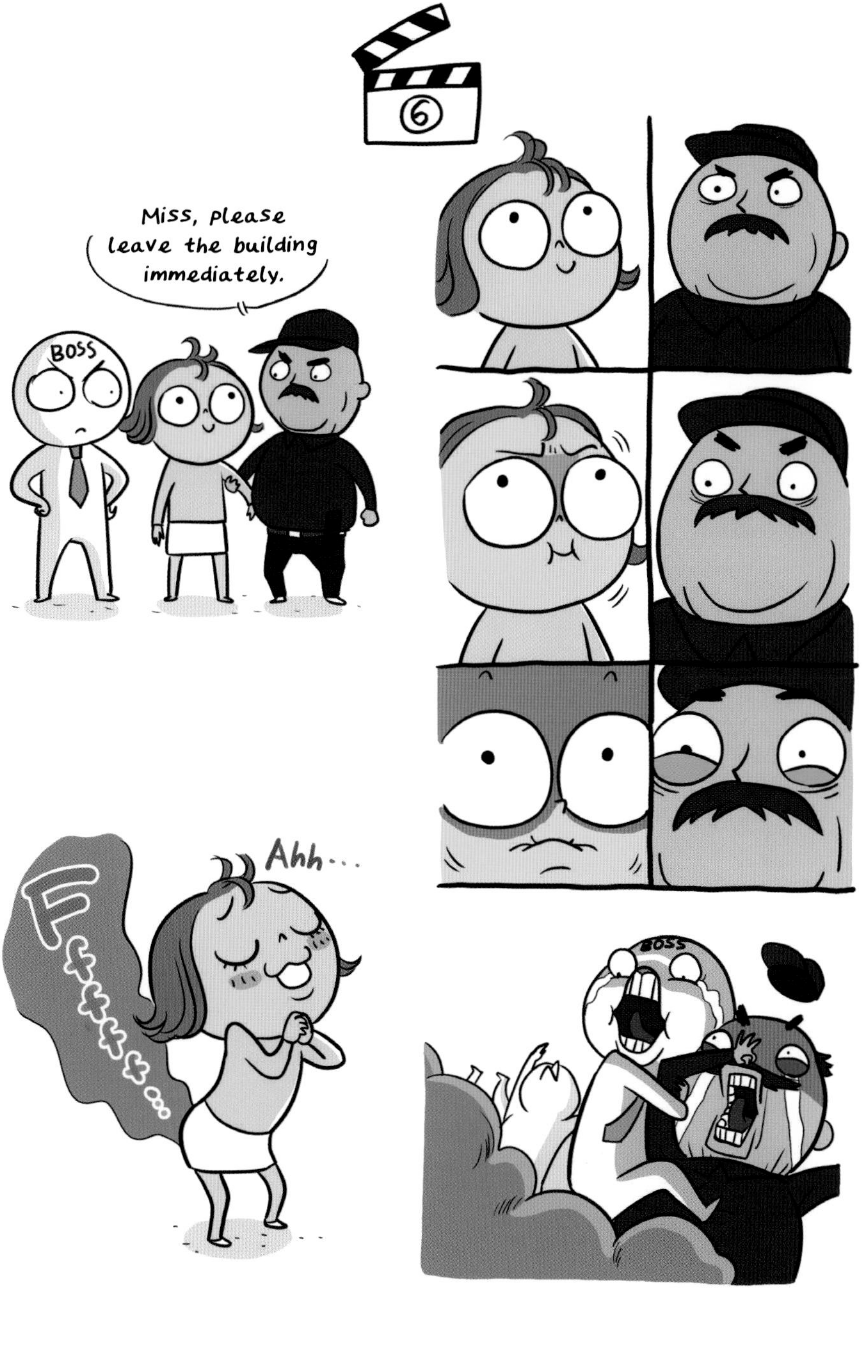
6
Miss, please leave the building immediately.
BOSS
Ahh...
Fffff...
BOSS

I'm a travel blogger.
I've been to 42 countries.

I'm a food blogger.
I've eaten at 587
restaurants.

I'm a fashion blogger.
I've owned thousands of
clothing and shoes.

I'm a parenting blogger.
I have only two kids.

Hubby...

I suddenly need
to go out
to do things.

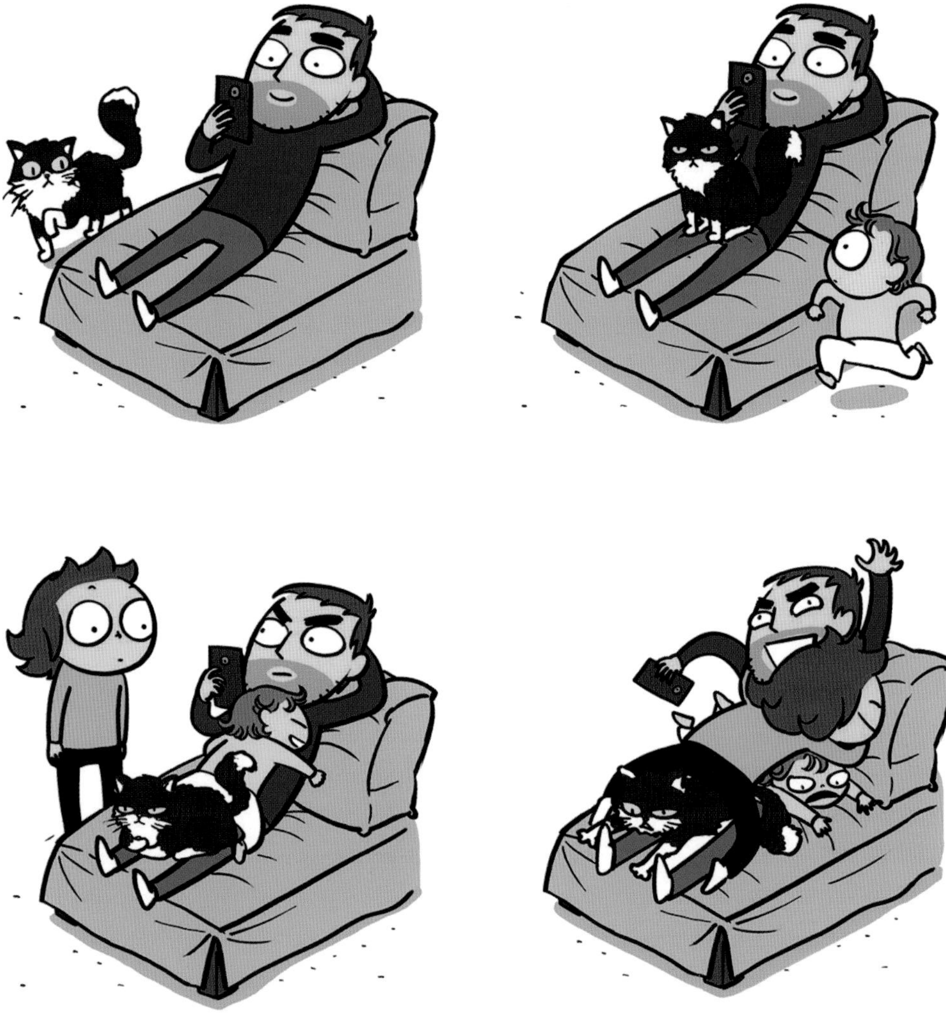

GOING TO THE BATHROOM WITH MY PHONE

A MINI VACATION

GOING TO THE BATHROOM WITHOUT MY PHONE

A SHORT-TERM CONFINEMENT

AFTER FINISHING MY MEAL

I've fueled my body with the right amount of energy like a responsible adult.

AFTER FINISHING MY CHILDREN'S LEFTOVERS

I'm about to explode...

Mommy, is Santa real?

Well, of cour—

FIVE YEARS LATER...

Why did you lie to me?

Santa is a fictional character, just like the Easter Bunny and the Little Mermaid. But we still enjoy the story, right?

TWO YEARS LATER...

My friends told me Santa IS real! Why did you lie to me?

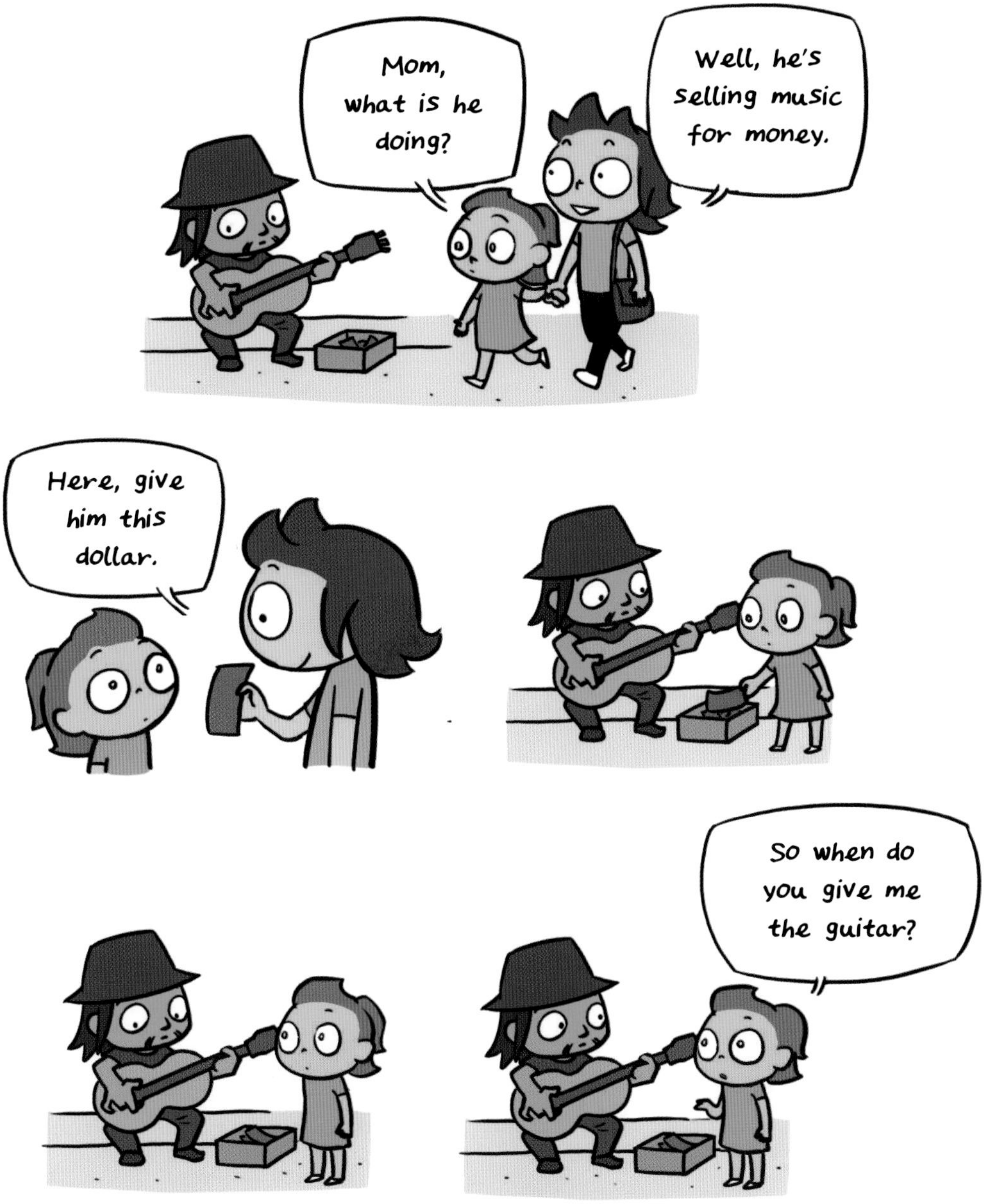
Mom, what is he doing?
Well, he's selling music for money.
Here, give him this dollar.
So when do you give me the guitar?

WHEN I BUY CLOTHES

The fit is a bit snug and I already have five similar jackets.

But I really like the buttons!

I'm so cute!

I will take both colors!

WHEN MY HUSBAND BUYS CLOTHES

ALI IS AWAKE AND
READY TO PLAY!

WHICH OF THE ABUNDANT
SUPPLY OF TOYS WILL ENGAGE
HER INTEREST TODAY?

THE GIANT BOX OF
COLORFUL LEGOS?

THE FUN, EXCITING RC CAR?

THE SHINY, FANCY
PRINCESS DOLLHOUSE?

OR THE ORDINARY,
DIRTY **TWIG** IN HER
SISTER'S HANDS?

BEING ON THE PHONE AT THE PLAYGROUND

BEING ON THE LAPTOP AT THE PLAYGROUND

Look at what I've got, a big chunk of time! I'm going to make the most of it!

MUNCH

MUNCH

It's OK. You can still give the rest to me.

IMPORTANT & MEANINGFUL THINGS

TANT & INGFUL GS

NETFLIX & MEMES

129

The sunny days are great.

It's fun, healthy, and lively.

But the rainy days...

You get to go out walking, hiking, biking, playing ball...

...are way better,

because you get to stay INSIDE, guilt-free.

plip

ploop

plip

plip

Sorry, guys, can't go out today.

It's OK.

ploop

Sure.

I CAN'T SLEEP
Baby, let's talk about CARS.
FIVE MINUTES LATER ...
Porsche's turbo engine ... I prefer the driving experience ... Google's self-driving technology ... compared with Tesla ... BMW's new model ... Audi ...
ZZzz...

MOMS IN A GROUP CHAT

Ladies, what do we want?
Fun for ourselves!
More girls' nights out!
Leaving the kids with their dads!
When do we want it?
...Well this weekend isn't good.
Hmm, I can't do anything on weekdays ...
...Let me check with my husband and get back ...

What's the best day of your life?

When you told me you were proud of me on my graduation, Mom.

What's the best day of your life?

The day we got married of course, honey.

What's the best day of your life?

It has to be the day when you were born, sweetie.

THE BEST DAY OF MY LIFE

Mom, husband, and kids have all gone out.

So quiet.

POOR BABIES! I WISH I WAS
THE SICK ONE.

I WAS SO WRONG.

AFTER A GOOD NIGHT'S SLEEP

I love my LIFE,
I love EVERYONE,
I love the WORLD!

AFTER A BAD NIGHT'S SLEEP

You offend me with
the way you breathe.

135

FIVE MINUTES LATER

Hold still!
Here we go...

Mommy,
I can do it.

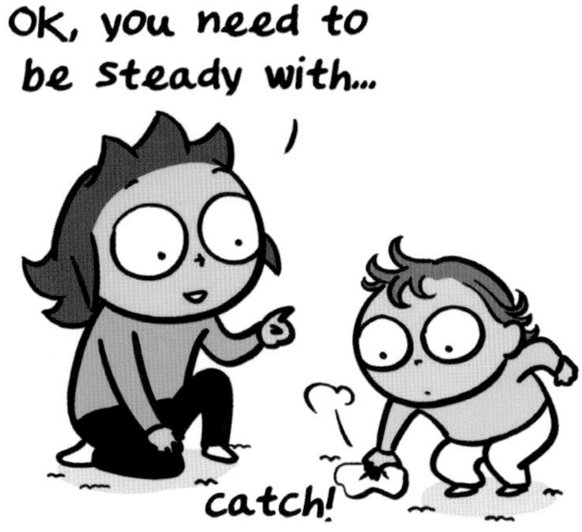

OK, you need to be steady with...
catch!

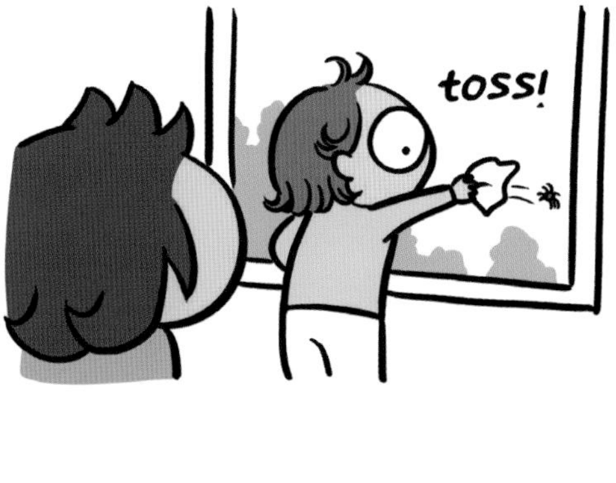

toss!

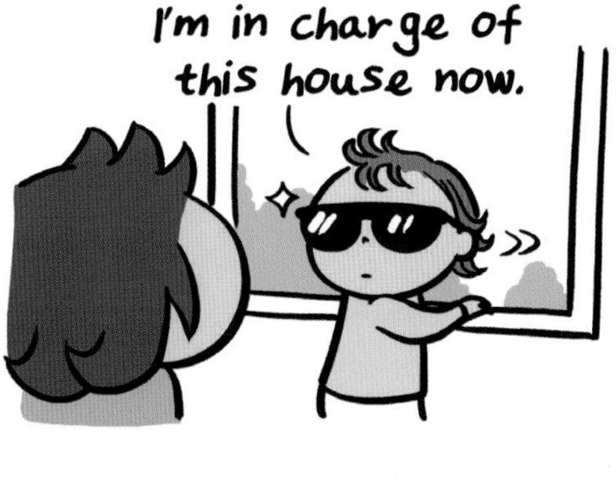

I'm in charge of this house now.

Hope you enjoyed the story of my family. See you next time!